Baking Made Easy

LORRAINE PASCALE

Baking Made Easy
LORRAINE PASCALE

100 fabulous,
easy to bake recipes

HarperCollins*Publishers*

HarperCollins*Publishers*
77–85 Fulham Palace Road,
London, W6 8JB
www.harpercollins.co.uk

First published by HarperCollins in 2011

14 13 12 11

9 8 7 6

Lorraine Pascale asserts her moral right to be
identified as the author of this work.

Text © Lorraine Pascale, 2011
Photographs © Myles New, 2011

ISBN 978-0-00-727594-6

Design: **'OME DESIGN**

Home Economy: Lorna Brash
Styling: Rachel Jukes
Printed and bound in Italy by L.E.G.O. S.p.A.

A catalogue record for this book is available
from the British Library.

This book accompanies the BBC TWO series,
Baking Made Easy.

BBC logo is copyright and trademark of the
British Broadcasting Corporation and is used
under licence.

The TV series was produced for BBC Television
by Pacific Productions.

Pacific
5-7 Anglers Lane
London
NW5 3DG
Tel: (+44) 207 691 2225
www.pacific.uk.com

Contents

Introduction

My earliest baking memory is one of me at primary school. I am five and carrying a battered old tin which contains the precious ingredients to make raspberry buns. My cookery teacher is an unexpectedly beautiful woman who looks like Marilyn Monroe. In those days, we had to provide all the ingredients – and we loved to mix and whisk vigorously – just like grown ups. We'd end up with these little rock-hard balls of dough that we'd artfully filled with raspberry jam. What an amazing feat to bake something all by yourself and then to eat it and share it proudly with your family. This was the first time I remember really appreciating food – and it was all down to baking. These classes only came round once a term but I looked forward to them more than anything else. So it was inevitable that my first cookery book would have an emphasis on baking. Writing this book really is a dream come true for me.

My heroes have always been the great female food writers Elizabeth David, Fanny Cradock, Isabella Beeton and Marguerite Patten – all extraordinary culinary visionaries whose influences are still prevalent today. Just like them, I have always wanted to find that 'work thing' I could feel passionate about. I enjoyed my modelling days, but I knew that it wasn't the thing I was destined to do for ever. I was briefly a secretary, then a mechanic, an interior designer – I even wrote a book about football's offside rule! But nothing held my attention for long. And then, by chance, I enrolled on a diploma cookery course at Leith's School and I knew at once I was home.

I had fallen head over heels. Friends readied themselves to tease me yet again about another failed venture but this time I surprised them all. I just kept on going with the course and I ended up studying cookery, specialising in patisserie, for over a decade. I cut my teeth working in some of the country's most respected kitchens and I worked alongside chefs who were completely committed to the pursuit of culinary perfection.

Looking back at my life, with its inevitable highs and lows, I now realise that I have always found a sense of purpose and a strength of mind when I am in the kitchen. The phone will ring and dramas will unfold outside, but cooking is where I find my peace and quiet. Time feels like it's standing still when actually it is flying by. I believe this is called being 'in the flow' – when you are so passionately and happily engaged in an activity that you lose all track of time.

In my first book I wanted to offer a series of recipes to showcase the magical chemistry of baking. Recipes that would stimulate the most sophisticated of palates, but also inspire those of less-experienced bakers. My book contains a hundred of my favourites and includes both sweet and savoury, from Fig, Cream Cheese & Mint Tart and White Chocolate Pannacotta, to Trout en Papillote with Sauterne and Almonds. There's my take on the Doris Grant Loaf, a delicious Gorgonzola & Pear Soufflé, my famous Stout & Stilton Bread Rolls, and a very wicked 'I just don't give a damn' Chocolate Cake. There are simpler ideas too, like my Glam Mac & Cheese and some Totally Lazy Sausage Rolls.

I have included a whole chapter of bread recipes, because I love making bread. It must be the physical process of rhythmically kneading a compliant dough that makes it one of the most therapeutic of activities. There is an almost religious experience to be had from thoughtfully crafting a loaf and then eating it warm from the oven. Think of delightfully aromatic foccacia from Italy – salty, oily and fragrant, or a sophisticated and discerning French fougasse that is mature enough to support the flavours of molten cheese and piquant ham. Crumbly and cake-like Irish soda bread, slapped with really good butter: I dream about this. With bread, the possibilities are limitless and I've included new twists on many favourites.

My book would not be complete without plenty of recipes devoted to a very special ingredient – chocolate. A product so universally adored, debated and eaten deserves special attention. I wanted to give you recipes that were delightful to prepare, beautiful to gaze at, dreamy to eat. Chocolate Melting Puddings and the Chocolate & Hazelnut Tart tick all the boxes, and there's my glorious 'I can't believe you made that cake', a mountain of chocolate cigarillos and strawberries. For all true chocolate brownie aficionados, I believe I have formulated the perfect recipe – a brownie that is light in texture, high in taste and substantial in the eating.

I hope I have written a book that will stand the test of time. A book that you will not only look at and admire, but will use, again and again and again. A book that comprehensively covers all the classics, but dares to give them a twist, that sits between practical and inspiring. These recipes will take you comfortably from Monday to Friday – with enough treats besides for special occasions and those precious weekends.

Have I inspired you? I sincerely hope so. Shake out your apron, switch off that phone, shut the kitchen door firmly and ramp up the music … because now is all about baking!

Lorraine's Baking Tips

Choosing your ingredients

Medium-sized eggs are used in all my recipes. A whole medium-sized egg weighs approximately 55g (2oz). A medium egg white weighs approx. 30g (1oz). So if you only have eggs of a different size in your kitchen, crack them into a jug and mix well, then measure out 55g for each whole egg required.

Most of my recipes use unsalted butter. However, a good-quality salted butter is okay to use (beware – the cheaper the butter, the more salt it contains). If using salted butter in cakes, omit any extra pinches of salt that are requested in the recipes.

I rarely use self-raising flour. Instead, I use plain flour and baking powder, which gives you more control over how much the cake will rise.

A good vanilla extract can make all the difference to a recipe, but for the best taste, use the seeds from actual vanilla pods. These are extremely expensive in the supermarkets, so if you do lots of baking, vanilla pods can be purchased in bulk on the internet. Instead of paying £3 for just two pods, buying in bulk can work out at as little as 12p per pod!

I never buy unwaxed lemons as they are so expensive, and not always readily available. For zest, buy ordinary lemons and wash them well in hot, soapy water. Give them a good rinse, rub them dry and the waxy coating will come off.

Tips for better baking

• Preheat your oven prior to weighing out any ingredients.

• Have all ingredients at room temperature for the best results, apart from when you need egg whites. Warm eggs are much harder to separate than cold ones, so cold, fresh eggs are best.

• Take your butter out of the fridge as soon as you get an urge to bake, as so many of my recipes call for soft butter. I've tried all sorts of not-so-clever quick melting solutions for too-hard butter, such as sitting it on a radiator, or placing it near the stove, but the one I fell in love with was grating it with a cheese grater into a bowl. The butter becomes instantly soft and ready to use. Genius!

• There is no need to sift flour, unless it has really clumped together or the recipe specifically states it.

• Icing sugar is normally best sifted as it does tend to clump together and may leave lumps in your buttercream.

• If possible, invest in some proper measuring spoons – a teaspoon and tablespoon are most commonly needed. These are available in most bigger supermarkets, from cookshops or online.

• When folding ingredients together, the best tool is a plastic spatula rather than a metal spoon (although this will do). Always fold the mixture slowly to retain as much air as possible.

• For safe and effective chopping, put a damp kitchen cloth underneath your chopping board to stop it sliding around.

• If attempting a pastry recipe, be aware that they aren't the fastest recipes in the world and due to their precise nature should not be hurried. Leave yourself plenty of time.

• When flouring a board or surface for rolling pastry, make sure there's enough flour to prevent the pastry sticking, but don't use so much that it changes the quantities of the recipe!

• For best results, do use the size of tin or dish recommended in the recipe.

• The best way to grease tins and pans is with the vegetable oil spray often used for low-fat frying.

• Bake cakes on the middle shelf of the oven at 180°C (350°F), Gas Mark 4 unless the recipe states otherwise. Bread should be baked in the top third of the oven, while meringues need to be put near the bottom. (For meringues, you can also leave the oven door open just a fraction, which allows moisture to escape.)

• Every oven is different, so cooking times can often vary. If opening the oven to check something's cooked, open the door, take out the item and then close the oven again quickly so that the heat does not get lost.

• To test if a cake is cooked, insert a skewer or cocktail stick into the centre of the cake – it should come out clean.

Tips for great bread-making

• If you do it right, bread-making can be the easiest thing in the world. For the very best loaves, fresh yeast is the way forward. But after it proved a challenge to buy in central London, I thought it prudent to suggest fast-action dried yeast for the recipes in this book. I know many people might have a bread maker – indeed, I was the owner of one for a spell – but I missed the tactile and magical experience that comes with being able to see every stage of the bread-making process, and I'm now a firm believer in making it by hand.

• Be brave with the water: the wetter the dough, the fluffier and lighter the loaf will be.

• Always measure out the salt precisely, as this one ingredient makes all the difference between a good-tasting loaf and a bad one. And be warned that lo-salt, whilst brilliant for other dishes, does not work well when making bread, because it doesn't impart enough flavour and the bread will end up tasting bland.

• Accurately time the kneading process and knead the dough for the full time stated in the recipe. It really does make a difference.

• When leaving the bread to rise, it likes to be in a warm but not hot place. Most airing cupboards and tops of radiators are too warm. A warm, cosy kitchen is usually just fine.

• To test if the bread has risen enough, flour your finger and gently prod the side of the loaf. When ready, the dough should spring halfway back up.

• Once a loaf is ready to bake, there are a number of ways to 'glaze' it. Milk will give it a soft, matt look; eggwash will give a shiny, crunchy look; and sieving a little flour over the top will give it an authentic rustic 'French bread' look.

• Try to create a steamy environment inside the oven – this will give the bread plenty of time to rise up before the hard crust starts to develop. Throw some ice cubes into the bottom of the oven, use a water spray to create a mist, or put a roasting tin, half filled with water, on the bottom shelf.

• If the top of your loaf is done but the bottom is not (to check, turn it over and tap it. If ready, it will sound hollow), cover the loaf loosely with some foil to prevent it from colouring further while it finishes cooking.

Breads

If you're lucky enough to live near a good patisserie or deli, you'll know what an amazing array of breads they have on show. When I have time, I find great comfort in making my own bread, and whether you're a novice or are well-practised in bread-making, there will be something for you here. Soda bread comes top for ease of making, while the fougasse needs slightly more effort and skill. Whichever recipes you choose, if you follow the instructions to the letter, you'll end up with a loaf to be proud of.

'Blues is to jazz what yeast is to bread. Without it, it's flat.'

Carmen McRae
Jazz vocalist and pianist
1920 – 1994

Croissants

A humble breakfast pastry or the king of Parisian patisserie – how did the simple croissant become so famous? The homemade version is quite different to the ones widely available in supermarkets. Admittedly there is a high degree of fiddlyness required to create this most perfect of crescent-shaped delights (and let's not dwell on the mountain of butter involved …). However, my recipe is speedier than other croissant recipes and the taste and texture are in sharp contrast to the soft, insipid variety you will have previously eaten. Makes 12–14

310g (11oz) strong white bread flour

165g (5½oz) plain flour, plus extra for dusting

2 tsp salt

60g (2½oz) soft light brown sugar

1 x 7g sachet of fast-action dried yeast

40g (1½oz) butter

250ml (9fl oz) water

230g (8¼oz) block of butter, softened

Vegetable oil or oil spray, for oiling

1 egg, lightly beaten, for glazing

Put the flours, salt, sugar, yeast and butter in a large bowl. Using your fingers, rub the butter into the mixture until it resembles fine breadcrumbs. Add the water and stir with a knife to bring the mixture together. Gently knead for less than a minute to a smooth ball. For croissants, unlike most bread, it is important that the dough is 'worked' as little as possible at this stage. Wrap it in clingfilm and leave in the fridge for 1 hour to rest.

Once the dough has been 'rested', roll it out on a well-floured surface to a rectangle no larger than 20 x 20cm (8 x 8in). Place the block of softened butter in the middle of the dough. The butter needs to be the same softness as the dough. Fold up the edges of the dough over the top so they overlap and completely cover the butter.

This next process is called rolling and folding, or 'turns', and it creates the characteristic flaky layers of a croissant. Keep the work surface well floured so the dough does not stick. Roll out the dough to a rectangle 3 times as long as it is wide, about 45 x 15cm (17¾ x 6in). Make sure it is rolled uniformly so the butter is spread out evenly inside.

Place the dough with the shortest end facing you. As if you were about to step out on a red carpet. Take the end nearest you and fold it into the centre. Then fold the top third down so the two ends now meet in the middle. Turn the dough 90° to the left and then repeat this step. Wrap the dough in clingfilm and put in the fridge for an hour to rest. You have now given the dough two 'rolls and folds'.

Remove the dough from the fridge and give the dough one more 'roll

▶

Croissants *(cont.)*

and fold' by rolling it out to 45 x 15cm (17¾ x 6in) again and folding the ends into the middle as before. Then roll it out to a rectangle about 35 x 14cm (14 x 5½in). Place the dough on the baking tray, cover with oiled clingfilm and leave to rest in the fridge for 1 hour.

Put the dough on a lightly floured work surface and trim any ragged edges with a sharp knife, then cut the dough in half lengthways. Cut each strip into triangles, each with a base of about 6cm (2½in) and two longer sides, 8.5 x 8.5cm (3⅓ x 3⅓in), going up to the point. You may have some trimmings left over. Place each triangle on the work surface with the longer point towards you and roll up the triangle away from you so that the tip folds over the top. Place them all on the baking tray and carefully curve into crescent shapes. Make sure the croissants are spaced well apart to allow them to expand during cooking. Cover with oiled clingfilm and leave to rise in a warm place for 1 hour.

Preheat the oven to 200°C (400°F), Gas Mark 6.

Brush the croissants lightly with the lightly beaten egg and bake in the oven for 15 minutes, or until golden brown. Remove from the oven and leave to cool on a wire rack.

Mascarpone & brown sugar
Scones

The unusual use of mascarpone and light brown sugar in this recipe makes these scones extra rich and a cut above the regular type. Makes 9

340g (12oz) self-raising flour, plus extra for dusting

1 tsp baking powder

Pinch of salt

80g (3oz) butter, cold and cubed

2 tbsp soft light brown sugar

80g (3oz) mascarpone

About 90ml (3fl oz) milk

1 egg, lightly beaten, for glazing

Preheat the oven to 210°C (415°F), Gas Mark 6–7. Dust a large baking tray with flour.

Put the flour, baking powder, salt, butter and sugar in a food processor and pulse until the mixture resembles breadcrumbs. Add the mascarpone, then pulse again for 3 seconds. (If you don't have a food processor, put all the ingredients in a medium bowl, pick up chunks of butter covered in flour and rub them between your thumbs and forefingers. Add the mascarpone and continue 'rubbing in'. This shouldn't take more than about 5 minutes.)

Pour the mixture into a large bowl and make a hole in the centre, then pour in enough milk to make a soft dough and stir with a knife. Use both hands to bring the mixture together, and squeeze, making sure any dry bits get picked up. It may seem like a crumbled mess but keep squeezing and the dough will come together. Knead lightly for a few seconds just to make the dough smooth and then roll out quickly on a lightly floured surface to about 2cm (¾in) thick.

Cut out rounds using a 6cm (2½in) round cutter (though any size will do) and place them on the prepared baking tray. It's important not to twist the cutter whilst doing this or the scones won't rise evenly when baked. Squish together any leftover dough, roll out and cut out more scones.

Brush the tops with beaten egg and bake in the oven for 10–12 minutes, or until the scones are nicely risen, firm and golden brown. Remove from the oven and leave to cool a little on the tray. They are best served fresh and warm from the oven with lashings of clotted cream, strawberry jam and a pot of tea.

Brioche Rolls

The easiest way to make brioche is in an electric mixer with a dough hook. You can make it by hand, but you'll need some time and a whole heap of patience. As an alternative to a brioche mould you can use a deep muffin tin. For a variation, soak some raisins in Madeira for an hour, dry them well, toss in flour (to stop them from sinking during baking) then add them to the dough once all the butter has been added. Makes 12

Vegetable oil or spray oil, for oiling

500g (1lb 2oz) plain flour, plus extra for dusting

1½ sachets of fast-action dried yeast (10g/⅓oz)

2 tsp salt

3 tbsp soft light brown sugar

6 cold eggs, lightly beaten

310g (11oz) butter, softened

1 egg, lightly beaten, for glazing

Equipment

12 mini brioche moulds or a 12-hole deep muffin or cupcake tin

Oil the moulds or muffin or cupcake tin.

Put the flour in an electric mixer with the yeast, salt and sugar. Add the eggs, two at a time, mixing well between each addition on a slow speed. Once the eggs are all added, mix for 8 minutes. With the mixer still on a low speed add the butter in 5 additions, making sure that each bit of butter is well mixed in before the next is added. Every couple of minutes or so, scrape the sides of the bowl down with a spatula to make sure that all of the dough is fully mixed in. This process of adding the butter takes a good 10 minutes on the machine. The mixture will go from a stiff ball of stretchy hopelessness to something silky and smooth once all the butter is incorporated.

Once all the butter has been added keep mixing it until the dough no longer sticks to the side of the mixing bowl.

If you are doing this by hand the dough will look like a big runny sticky mess initially and keep sticking badly to the work surface. Just keep pulling the dough up and then pushing it down and scraping it off the work surface so you are continuously stretching and moving it. Eventually the dough will become less sticky, more elastic and begin to be a little easier to handle. It is tempting to throw in more flour so that it is less sticky, but doing this will change the brioche recipe altogether and make it more like regular bread. This may take up to 20–25 minutes or more. The dough will still be very soft at this stage.

▶

Brioche rolls *(cont.)*

Once the dough is ready, divide it into a third and two-thirds. Take the larger piece and divide it into 12 equal pieces. With well-floured hands take one of the pieces and make a ball with it, push it down into the mould or tin, then with a floured finger make a big hole in the middle. Repeat with the rest of this piece of dough. Then take the smaller third piece and break it into 12 portions. Roll each one into a bullet shape so it has a round ball at the top and a long pointed end. Push the pointed end into the hole all the way down so only the top third of the bullet is showing. Repeat with the rest of the dough. Alternatively, if by this stage you have had enough of your brioche, which, believe me, can happen, you can freeze it for up to a month by wrapping in clingfilm or putting it into a freezerproof bag and come back to it another day once it is defrosted and you are ready to conquer it again.

Oil the top of the bread and cover loosely with clingfilm, making sure it is airtight. Leave in a warm place until the dough has almost doubled in size, about 2–3 hours (this takes longer than other breads due to the high fat content).

Preheat the oven to 200°C (400°F), Gas Mark 6.

Once risen, remove the clingfilm and brush the dough well with the lightly beaten egg. Place in the top half of the oven, making sure there is room for the brioche to rise, and bake for about 35 minutes, or until the brioche is a rich golden brown and comes out of the moulds or tin easily. Take a peek after about 20 minutes of cooking. If you feel that the top is getting too dark, just cover the brioche with some baking paper to give the centre a chance to cook without any further browning to the surface. Remove the brioche from the oven and leave to cool in the tin.

Brioche has many uses. It makes an enticing breakfast bread, especially when spread with butter and served warm. Sliced, it can be served with foie gras and a rich chutney. For an extra special pud, make a large brioche and use it to make a bread and butter pudding.

Spiced fruit
Tea Loaf

A traditional English tea bread, spiked with spices and dried fruit.

Makes 1 small loaf

Vegetable oil or oil spray, for oiling

180g (6½oz) strong white bread flour

180g (6½oz) plain flour, plus extra for dusting

1 tbsp ground ginger

1 tbsp ground cinnamon

1 x 7g sachet of fast-action dried yeast

1 tbsp soft light brown sugar

1 tsp salt

Grated zest of 1 lemon

1 egg, plus 1 egg, lightly beaten, for glazing

1 tbsp treacle

150ml (5fl oz) warm water

80g (3oz) sultanas

60g (2½oz) dates, chopped

Equipment

22 x 10cm (8¾ x 4in) loaf tin

Oil and line the loaf tin with baking paper.

Put the flours, ginger, cinnamon, yeast, sugar, salt and lemon zest in a medium bowl. Make a hole in the centre and pour in the egg, treacle and warm water. Mix to a soft dough, then transfer to a floured work surface and knead the dough for 10 minutes by hand or for 5 minutes in an electric mixer fitted with a dough hook. This dough is quite wet, which makes for a lighter loaf but can be tricky to knead initially. The more it is kneaded the less sticky it will get. Try not to add any more flour.

Once the dough is kneaded, plop it back in a bowl (if you are doing it by hand), or if using a machine remove the bowl (with the bread still in it) from the machine. Add the sultanas and dates. Knead the bread in the bowl for 1 minute to make sure all the fruit is evenly distributed. Then shape into a ball and plop it into the prepared loaf tin.

Squish the bread down at the corners slightly and then cover loosely with clingfilm, making sure it is airtight. Leave in a warm place until the bread has almost doubled in size.

Preheat the oven to 200°C (400°F), Gas Mark 6.

Once the dough is well risen, brush with the beaten egg and bake in the oven for 30–40 minutes, or until golden brown and well risen. Using oven gloves, remove the bread from the tin and check that the underside is also cooked, it should sound hollow when tapped. If not, pop the loaf back in the oven without the tin for another 5 minutes.

Remove from the oven and leave to cool on a wire rack. Serve warm or cold at 4pm with jam and tea.

Almond, honey & orange
Kugelhopf

Kugelhopf, Gougelhopf and Gugelhupf are a few of the many spelling variations of this recipe from Alsace in eastern France. A cakelike bread, it is traditionally served as part of a Sunday breakfast feast, but is also wonderful eaten in the evening with a glass of ambrosial wine. Makes 1 loaf

Vegetable oil, for oiling

450g (16oz) strong white bread flour, plus extra for dusting

110g (4oz) dried apricots, finely chopped (easiest to cut with scissors)

250ml (9fl oz or 1 wine glass) builder's tea or orange liqueur

100g (3½oz) ground almonds

1½ sachets of fast-action dried yeast (about 10g/⅓oz)

1 tsp ground cinnamon

2 tsp salt

2 tbsp soft light brown sugar

Grated zest of 2 large oranges

180ml (6½fl oz) warm milk

3 eggs, beaten

160g (5½oz) butter, melted

2 big squidges of honey

Handful of whole skinless almonds

Icing sugar, for sprinkling

Equipment

Large kugelhopf mould

Oil the kugelhopf mould, then dust with flour and set aside.

Put the apricots in a bowl, add the tea or orange liqueur and leave to stand for 30 minutes. Put the flour in another large bowl with the ground almonds, yeast, cinnamon, salt, sugar and orange zest. In a third bowl, mix together the milk, eggs, butter and honey.

Add enough of the butter mix to the flour mixture to make a soft dough. The dough will be softer than most other doughs but it should not be too sticky. Knead the dough for 10 minutes by hand on a lightly floured work surface or for 5 minutes in an electric mixer fitted with a dough hook, then set aside.

Drain the apricots and add them to the dough. Fold the dough over itself 3–4 times until the apricots are evenly dispersed throughout the dough.

Place an almond into each 'dip' of the kugelhopf mould, then carefully make a hole in the middle of the dough and squish it gently into the prepared mould. Cover the top loosely with oiled clingfilm, making sure it is airtight. Leave in a warm place until the dough has doubled in size. This will take about 1 hour or so, depending on the warmth of the room.

Preheat the oven to 200°C (400°F), Gas Mark 6.

Bake the kugelhopf in the oven for about 35 minutes, or until it is golden brown and comes out of the mould easily. Remove the bread from the mould, place on a baking tray and pop back into the oven for 5–10 minutes to brown up the base.

Remove the bread from the oven and leave to cool. Once cooled right down, sprinkle the top with icing sugar and serve.

Coffee & maple
Panettone

Panettone is an Italian bread usually made with fruit peel and traditionally eaten at Christmas. I wanted to make something a little away from the norm, so I came up with this tasty gem which uses a different mix of flavours. Makes 1 large panettone

560g (1¼lb) strong white bread flour

½ tsp salt

1½ sachets of fast-action dried yeast (about 10g/⅓oz)

200ml (7fl oz) warm milk

3 eggs

2 egg yolks

Seeds of 1 vanilla pod or 2 drops of vanilla extract

100ml (4fl oz) maple syrup, plus extra for drizzling

4 tbsp coffee essence or 1 tbsp coffee powder diluted in the milk mentioned above

200g (7oz) butter, melted

Eggwash

1 egg

1 tbsp milk

Equipment

18cm (7in) deep loose-bottomed cake tin

Preheat the oven to 200°C (400°F), Gas Mark 6. Line the sides of the cake tin with baking paper, so it sticks up a good 10cm (4in) above the top of the tin.

Put flour, salt, yeast, milk, eggs, yolks, vanilla, maple syrup, coffee and butter in a large bowl and stir well to combine. Keep mixing the dough for 10 minutes by hand (it is usually too sticky for the hand at first so use a wooden spoon and keep mixing), or for 5 minutes if using an electric mixer fitted with a dough hook. The dough will be very very sticky, almost like a cake batter. This is what gives the panettone its wonderful spongy texture.

Tip the dough into the prepared cake tin and lay a tea towel gently over the top. Leave in a warm place for about 1 hour, or until the mixture has almost risen to the top of the tin.

For the eggwash, mix the egg and milk together in a bowl. Once the dough has almost doubled in size, brush the top of the panettone with the eggwash, then make a cross in the top with a very sharp knife. Bake in the oven for 45–50 minutes, or until the bread is well risen, lifts out of the tin easily and a skewer inserted into the thickest part comes out clean.

Remove the panettone from the oven, drizzle with maple syrup and use a brush to spread it evenly over the bread. This gives the loaf a shiny top and adds extra maple flavour. Leave the panettone to cool in the tin.

Variation The coffee can be omitted and replaced with 400g (14oz) mixed dried fruit and peel soaked in orange juice or rum. This turns it into a more traditional panettone.

Focaccia Bread

Great for sharing, and made even better with the use of a really fine extra-virgin olive oil. I keep a good bottle of extra-virgin on the top shelf of a cupboard, away from prying hands who may want to use the oil for frying eggs or other unworthy cooking tasks. On special occasions, such as making focaccia, the imperial bottle of oil makes a rare appearance. Makes 1 large flat loaf

500g (1lb 2oz) strong white bread flour, plus extra for dusting

2 tsp salt

1 x 7g sachet of fast-action dried yeast

80ml (3fl oz) olive oil, plus extra for drizzling

150–250ml (5–9fl oz) warm water

Vegetable oil or oil spray, for oiling

1 bunch of fresh rosemary

Large pinch of sea salt

Dust a large flat baking tray with flour.

Put the flour in a large bowl, add the salt and yeast, then add the olive oil plus enough warm water to make a soft but not sticky dough. The dough should feel quite loose and not tight and difficult to knead. If the whole amount is added it may appear that the dough is beyond repair, but gently kneading by way of scooping up the dough, scraping any sticky bits on the surface and slapping it back down again for a few minutes will see the dough begin to become 'pillowy' and more manageable. The more water that can be added (the full 250ml/9fl oz is great) then the lighter the bread will be. But it can take some perseverance. Also resist the temptation to add more flour as it will make the dough too heavy.

Knead the dough for about 10 minutes by hand on a lightly floured work surface or for 5 minutes if using an electric mixer fitted with a dough hook. The dough will feel stretchy when pulled. To test if it is ready, make a ball with the dough then, using a well-floured finger, prod a shallow indent in the side (no more than ¾cm/¼in). If the indent disappears by way of the dough springing back then it is ready to shape. If the indent stays, knead for a few minutes longer.

Shape the dough into an oval and place it on the prepared baking tray. Flatten it out to about 30cm (12in) long and 20cm (8in) wide. Cover the dough loosely with oiled clingfilm, making sure it is airtight.

Preheat the oven to 200°C (400°F), Gas Mark 6.

▶

Focaccia bread *(cont.)*

Leave the dough in a warm place for about 1 hour, or until it has almost doubled in size. With a floured index finger press holes in the dough at regular intervals, about 4cm (1½in) apart in rows across the dough, pressing right down to the bottom. Take 3cm (1¼in) long sprigs of the rosemary and push them into the holes. Sprinkle some sea salt over the dough and place in the top third of the oven. Bake for about 25–30 minutes, or until the bread is well risen, light golden brown and feels hollow when tapped underneath.

Remove from the oven, drizzle with the remaining olive oil and leave to cool on the baking tray. This is totally awesome when served warm as a starter or indeed as a meal in itself with fresh tomatoes, artichokes and cold meats, or with a steaming hot bowl of soup.

Stout & Stilton
Bread Rolls

A bloke's bread. Malty stout loaves with strong, masculine Stilton. Lovely.
Makes 10 rolls

370g (13oz) strong white bread flour, plus extra for dusting

200g (7oz) wholemeal flour

Handful of fresh thyme leaves

1 tsp salt

1 x 7g sachet of fast-action dried yeast

200ml (7fl oz) stout (or apple juice), at room temperature

120–180ml (4–6fl oz) warm water

Vegetable oil or oil spray, for oiling

200g (7oz) Stilton, crumbled

Dust a large, flat baking tray with flour.

In a large bowl, mix the flours, thyme, salt and yeast together. Pour in the beer (or apple juice) and enough of the water to make a sticky dough. Stir everything together, then knead until smooth and elastic — about 10 minutes by hand on a lightly floured work surface or 5 minutes in an electric mixer fitted with a dough hook.

Divide the dough into 10 equal pieces. I weigh each piece to ensure everything is equal! Mine weigh 97g (3½oz) each (I use the full amount of water to make the dough). Shape each piece into an oval rugby-ball shape and place on the prepared baking tray, spaced about 8cm (3in) apart. Cover with oiled clingfilm, making sure it is airtight. Leave in a warm place until the rolls have doubled in size.

Preheat the oven to 200°C (400°F), Gas Mark 6.

Remove the clingfilm from the rolls and take a razor or extremely sharp knife, preferably serrated. Carefully slice each roll along its length to a depth of two-thirds of the bread. Spread the cut open quite a bit with your fingers, as when the bread bakes it will try to close up. Repeat with all the rolls. Crumble the Stilton into the slits, pull the bread around the cheese to prevent it spilling out in the oven, then bake for about 20 minutes, or until the rolls feel firm and sound hollow when tapped underneath. Remove the rolls from the oven and serve warm with a chutney or relish.

Big fat salt & pepper
Breadsticks

The best way to serve these breadsticks is with dips, such as hummus, taramasalata and guacamole. Mini sticks can be fun as canapés for a dinner party, or vary the toppings with fresh rosemary and thyme, or sesame and poppy seeds. Makes 12

450g (1lb) strong white bread flour, plus extra for dusting

1 x 7g sachet of fast-action dried yeast

1½ tsp salt

250–275ml (9–10fl oz) warm water

Vegetable oil or spray oil, for oiling

2 tbsp extra-virgin olive oil

2 tbsp sea salt

2 tbsp freshly ground black pepper

Dust two large baking trays with flour.

Put the flour, yeast and the 1½ teaspoons of salt into a large bowl and add enough of the water to make a soft but not sticky dough. Knead well for 10 minutes by hand on a lightly floured work surface or for 5 minutes if using an electric mixer fitted with a dough hook.

Divide the mixture into 12 equal portions, each weighing about 60g (2½oz). Roll them into balls, then place each ball on a floured surface and roll into a long sausage shape about 25 x 2cm (10 x 1in). For the best visual results make the sausage shape an even thickness.

I like to shape half of them into twists. Run a knife down the centre to split the dough, leaving a bit at the bottom uncut. Braid or plait the two halves over each other to give a twisted effect.

Place the breadsticks on the prepared baking trays, spacing them 4cm (1½in) apart.

Preheat the oven to 200°C (400°F), Gas Mark 6.

Cover the breadsticks loosely with oiled clingfilm, making sure it is airtight. Leave in warm place for 30 minutes, or until the breadsticks have almost doubled in size.

Remove the clingfilm and brush each breadstick with the extra-virgin olive oil. Sprinkle half the breadsticks with the sea salt and the remainder with the freshly ground black pepper. Bake on the top third of the oven for about 20 minutes, or until the breadsticks are lightly golden and feel firm to the touch. Remove the breadsticks from the oven and leave to cool on the baking trays.

Chorizo & thyme
Fougasse

Chorizo and thyme make a powerful flavour combination. Buy the big, thick chorizo sausage (either ready-to-eat or to be cooked), rather than slices, and cut into chunky pieces. A vegetarian in the house? Substitute the chorizo for a couple of handfuls of sun-dried tomatoes and sprinkle the top of the bread with some Parmesan cheese. Serves 6

500g (1lb 2oz) strong white bread flour, plus extra for dusting

2 tsp salt

2 tsp fast-action dried yeast

250–300ml (9–11fl oz) water

Leaves of 4 sprigs of fresh thyme

50g (2oz) ready-to-eat chorizo sausage, very finely chopped

Vegetable oil, for oiling

3 tbsp milk, for brushing

Preheat the oven to 200°C (400°F), Gas Mark 6. Dust a large baking tray with flour.

Put the flour, salt and yeast in a large bowl and mix together to combine. Make a large hole in the centre of the flour mix, then pour in the water, just enough to make a dough which is loose and easy to knead, but not too sticky. If it feels tight like Blue-tack then add more water. As you knead it, the dough will become less sticky, so if you can add all the 300ml (11fl oz) your loaf will be much lighter with a lovely open texture.

Knead the dough for 10 minutes by hand on a lightly floured work surface or for 5 minutes in an electric mixer fitted with a dough hook. Add the thyme and knead for a further 30 seconds, or until it is well combined. Put half the chorizo in the middle of the dough and then fold the edge around it to cover and knead it for an extra minute.

On a floured surface, shape the fougasse into a ball making sure the top of the ball is taught and smooth. Using a rolling pin, roll it out into a rough oval shape. Using a very sharp knife, or razor blade, carefully cut slashes in the loaf to look like a fern leaf, then with floured hands open up the slashes wide, as they will close up a lot when the bread is left to double in size.

Push the remaining chorizo into the top of the dough, then cover the dough loosely with oiled clingfilm (you may need several pieces). Leave to rise in a warm place until the dough has doubled in size.

▶

Chorizo & thyme fougasse *(cont.)*

Remove the clingfilm, brush the dough with milk and place in the oven. Throw a couple of handfuls of ice cubes in the bottom of the oven or spray the oven with water before closing. This will keep a crust from forming too quickly on the bread, which would prevent the bread from rising nicely. Alternatively, put a roasting tin with water in the bottom of the oven instead.

Bake for 30–35 minutes, or until the bread is well risen, a beautiful golden brown and smells wonderfully cooked. It will come off the tray once fully cooked too.

It is tough to top the taste of warm bread straight from the oven, slathered in oodles of good butter.

White Loaf

The process of making bread by hand is so rewarding. There is something therapeutic about kneading then shaping the loaf and leaving it in a warm place to grow. I confess I had a bread machine for a while, but I missed the comforting steps of the bread-making process, so I sold it online! This loaf has a soft crust and a perfectly pillowy centre. Angelic. Makes 1 loaf, two 23 x 12cm (9 x 4¾in) loaves or 12 rolls

560g (1¼lb) strong white bread flour, plus extra for dusting

1 tsp salt

1 x 7g sachet fast-action dried yeast

380ml (13fl oz) warm milk

1 squidge of honey

Vegetable oil or oil spray, for oiling

1 egg, lightly beaten, for glazing

Equipment

Two 23 x 12cm (9 x 4¾in) loaf tins or 1–2 large baking trays

Put the flour, salt and yeast in a large bowl. Make a hole in the centre and pour in the milk and honey. Mix well to combine, then knead for 10 minutes by hand on a lightly floured work surface or for 5 minutes in an electric mixer fitted with a dough hook. The dough may seem quite damp, but don't be tempted to add more flour, as the wetter the dough the lighter the loaf! Just keep kneading and it will become less sticky.

If using loaf tins, divide the dough into 2 balls, smooth the tops and plop each one into a tin. Squish the dough down at the corners slightly and cover loosely with oiled clingfilm, making sure it is airtight.

If you are doing a free-form loaf or dinner rolls, dust the baking tray(s) with flour. Shape the dough into a ball on a floured work surface or divide into 12 rolls, then put on the baking tray(s) and cover loosely with clingfilm, making sure it's airtight. Keeping the dough airtight encourages it to rise, but leaving the clingfilm loose gives the bread room to grow.

Leave to rise in a warm place until the dough has almost doubled in size.

Once the dough is well risen, carefully slash the top(s) with a sharp, serrated knife and preheat the oven to 200°C (400°F), Gas Mark 6. Brush the dough with the beaten egg and bake in the oven for about 30 minutes, or until the bread is golden brown and well risen. Using oven gloves, remove the loaves from the tins and check the undersides are cooked and the bases sound hollow when tapped. If still a little pale, place the bread back in the oven without the tins for 5–10 minutes.

Once cooked, leave the bread to cool on a wire rack. Serve with a good butter and our favourite yeasted spread!

Soda Bread

Perhaps the easiest bread to make by hand, with little kneading and no waiting around for it to rise. Treacle gives it an earthy taste, darkens the crumb and crisps up the crust. This recipe calls for buttermilk, available from bigger supermarkets; a homemade version can be made by putting lemon juice in regular milk and letting it sit for a few minutes. Makes 1 loaf

370g (13oz) plain flour, plus extra for dusting

130g (4½oz) wholemeal flour

1 tsp bicarbonate of soda

1 tsp salt

40g (1½oz) butter, melted

1 tbsp treacle

300–340ml (11–12fl oz) buttermilk, or warm milk plus 1 tbsp lemon juice (see intro)

Preheat the oven to 200°C (400°F), Gas Mark 6 and put the top shelf in position.

Place the flours, bicarbonate of soda and salt into a large bowl and stir together. Make a large hole in the centre of the flour mixture and pour in the melted butter and treacle plus enough of the buttermilk to make a loose sticky dough. The best way with treacle is to run the tablespoon under a really hot tap for 10 seconds before dipping it into the treacle. This ensures the treacle runs easily off the spoon and into the dough.

Tip the dough on to a lightly dusted work surface. The dough will be quite sticky. Knead the dough for 1 minute, then shape it into a large ball with a taut, smooth top. Place the dough on a baking tray and flatten it a bit. I find the easiest way to do this is with a rolling pin. Take a wooden spoon, put some flour over the whole handle then hold it horizontally over the bread. Put the wooden spoon handle on top of the bread then push it down until you feel the baking tray at the bottom. This mark is the first half of the trademark soda bread cross. Repeat with a line at right angles to this. Dust with some flour then bake in the oven for 30–40 minutes, or until the bread is brown, has risen nicely and the dough inside where the cross was made is not damp.

Serve fresh from the oven with butter and jam. This bread does not keep well so is best eaten on the day that it is baked – but if you have any left, it does make good toast.

Doris Grant
Loaf

A 'No-need-to-knead bread', adapted from a 1940s recipe by healthy-eating evangelist Doris Grant, who believed white flour – and its lack of nutrients – was the enemy. Making bread one day, Doris forgot to knead it. On tasting the loaf, she discovered it had a very fair taste and decided never again to bother kneading her bread. The resulting loaf is heavy but quicker to make than other types of bread. Makes 1 small loaf

225g (8oz) strong white bread flour, plus extra for dusting

225g (8oz) strong wholemeal flour

1 tsp salt

1 x 7g sachet of fast-action dried yeast

1 tbsp honey

300ml (11fl oz) warm water

Vegetable oil or oil spray, for oiling

A little milk, for brushing

Dust a medium baking tray with flour.

Sift the flours into a large bowl and reserve the grain – the brown bits that are too big to fit through the sieve. Add the salt and yeast, then make a big hole in the centre and pour in the honey and water. Mix well to form a smooth dough, working it gently with your hands if necessary. If the dough feels a bit stiff, add an extra 2 tablespoons of water. Shape into a ball and place on the prepared baking tray. Make sure the top is smooth and wrinkle-free. Cover the dough loosely with oiled clingfilm, making sure it is airtight, and leave to rise in a warm place for a good hour, or until it has almost doubled in size.

Preheat the oven to 200°C (400°F), Gas Mark 6. Remove the clingfilm from the dough and make a few slashes in the top with a sharp knife – I use a sharp serrated knife and saw gently. Brush the loaf with milk, sprinkle with the reserved grain, then place in the oven. Throw about 10 ice cubes into the bottom of the oven – they will produce steam, which keeps the crust from hardening too quickly. (A quickly hardened crust prevents the bread from rising well.) Bake the bread for 30–40 minutes, or until it has risen, sounds hollow when tapped underneath and comes easily off the baking tray. Remove from the oven and leave to cool on the tray. Eat as soon as it is cool enough.

Serve fresh from the oven with loads of butter. These loaves do not keep well. However, if the whole lot does not disappear in one sitting, slice up the remainder and put it in the freezer. When ready to eat, pull out a slice and pop it in the toaster. Breakfasts for the next few days…? Sorted.

Pumpkin & rosemary
Muffins

I wrote this in November, when pumpkins had been whisked away for Halloween, so I had to substitute a butternut squash. To cook a small amount of pumpkin, dice into cubes and place in a pan with just enough water to cover. Bring to the boil, lower the heat and pop on a lid, slightly askew. Boil/steam for 5–10 minutes and top up with water if needed. Drain and use. These muffins don't rise loads but they have a flavoursome, moist crumb. Makes 12 muffins

Vegetable oil or oil spray, for oiling

180g (6½oz) self-raising flour

130g (4½oz) wholemeal flour

1 tsp baking powder

½ tsp bicarbonate of soda

Good pinch of salt

3 sprigs of fresh rosemary, very finely chopped

240g (8½oz) cooked pumpkin (about 1 small wedge), cut into 0.5cm (¼in) dice. Ready-cubed, uncooked squash is available in the supermarket

2 eggs, lightly beaten

100ml (4fl oz) plain yogurt

275ml (10fl oz) milk

3 big squidges of honey

60ml (2½fl oz) vegetable oil

Handful of pumpkin seeds

Equipment
12-hole muffin tin

Preheat the oven to 200°C (400°F), Gas Mark 6.

Cut out 12 squares of baking paper measuring about 14 x 14cm (5½in). Oil the muffin tin and push the squares down into each hole so the paper sticks up just like the muffins you can buy in the coffee shop. The squares have a habit of popping up out of the holes, which is OK for now as once the muffin mix is spooned inside the squares will stay down. Alternatively, use ready-made paper muffin cases.

In a large bowl, sift the flours, baking powder and bicarbonate of soda, stir in the salt and rosemary. If there is any wholegrain left in the sieve from the wholemeal flour, keep this for the topping.

In a medium bowl, put the rest of the ingredients, apart from a third of the pumpkin, and stir well so all the liquid is well combined. Pour the wet ingredients into the dry and, using a large spoon and no more than 8 turns, mix all the ingredients together. It does not take much to over-mix muffins at this stage and although the end result will still taste sublime the texture will not be as tender. Leave the mixture to stand for 5 minutes, then spoon the mixture into the paper cases.

Sprinkle the wholegrain, reserved pumpkin and the pumpkin seeds over the muffins. Bake in the centre of the oven for 20–25 minutes, or until the muffins are well risen and a skewer inserted in the centre comes out clean.

Good for breakfast, good for lunch and good for just about any time of the day for a snack. For canapés these can made in mini muffin cases as mouthful morsels of scrumbunctiousness.

Cakes

For me, cakes say cosiness and contentment, home, warmth and love. Whatever the occasion, there's always room for a cake: there are 'just like mum would make' cakes, 'someone's getting wed' cakes, 'I don't give a damn' cakes and pretty little tea cakes. Most people's first baking memory is of making a cake, side by side with their mother, helping out but ultimately wishing she would be quick and put the cake in the oven so they could get on with licking that spoon or bowl.

'There is no love sincerer than the love of food.'

George Bernard Shaw
Playwright
1856 – 1950

My big fat
Carrot Cake

A no-holds-barred cake with three moist spiced layers of pure excess. If you don't fancy making this sky-high cake, which takes a whopping nine eggs, then knock off a third of the ingredients and make a more humble two-layer cake instead. Makes a three-tier 23cm (9in) round cake (V)

525ml (18½fl oz) vegetable oil

9 eggs, lightly beaten

525g (1lb 3oz) soft dark brown sugar

420g (15oz) carrots, peeled and grated

Grated zest of 3 large oranges

525g (1lb 3oz) self-raising flour

Pinch of salt

1 tbsp bicarbonate of soda

1½ tbsp mixed spice

Seeds of 1 vanilla pod or 2 drops vanilla extract

Cream cheese frosting

200g (7oz) icing sugar

40g (1½oz) butter, cubed

Finely grated zest of 1 lemon

Seeds of ½ vanilla pod or 1 drop vanilla extract

115g (4¼oz) low-fat cream cheese, chilled

Handful of pecans or walnuts, toasted to decorate

Equipment

Three x 23cm (9in) round tins

Preheat the oven to 180°C (325°F), Gas Mark 4. Prepare the tins by oiling the insides and lining the bases with baking paper.

Put the oil, eggs, sugar, carrots and orange zest in a large bowl and mix with a wooden spoon. If you're making all three tiers, you may have to do this in batches. Mix the flour, salt, bicarbonate of soda and mixed spice together, then sift into the bowl. Add the vanilla and lightly mix everything together until the mixture is uniform but still soft and runny. Ladle into the prepared tins and bake in the oven for 40–45 minutes. Ovens vary so have a peek after 30 minutes to see how the cakes are getting on. The cakes are ready when the sponge springs back up if pushed lightly. A skewer inserted into the middle should come out clean. Leave to cool for 5 minutes or so, then turn out onto a wire rack and peel off the paper.

For the cream cheese frosting, mix the icing sugar, butter, lemon zest and vanilla together in a bowl, then whisk well to combine. Stir in the cream cheese. If the mixture looks too runny, put it in the fridge for 10–12 minutes to harden up. When the cakes are cool, take two of them and use a large, sharp knife to slice off the domed tops, leaving them completely flat. Don't slice the top off the third cake.

Put a dollop of frosting in the middle of a serving plate or stand to stop the cake from sliding. Take one of the flattened cakes and place it on top. Then pop a big spoonful of frosting onto it and spread all over, leaving a 2.5cm (1in) gap around the edge so that the frosting does not squelch over too much when you add the next layer. Put the next flattened cake on top and repeat with more frosting. Put the unsliced tier on the top, cover generously with frosting and decorate with toasted nuts, if desired.

Banana Loaf
with rum & pecans

A classic flavour combination. I love the soft, woody flavours of pecans, but you could always use walnuts instead. Serves 6–8 (V)

Vegetable oil or oil spray, for oiling

Handful of pecans, plus a few to decorate

100g (3½oz) butter, softened

150g (5oz) soft light brown sugar

Seeds of 1 vanilla pod or 2 drops of vanilla extract

3 eggs

150g (5oz) plain flour

Pinch of salt

Generous pinch of ground cinnamon

1 heaped tsp baking powder

2 overripe bananas, slightly mashed

Rum sugar syrup

100ml (4fl oz) dark rum

100g (3½oz) soft light brown sugar

Equipment

22 x 10cm (8¾ x 4in) loaf tin

Preheat the oven to 170°C (325°F), Gas Mark 3. Oil the loaf tin then line with baking paper, making sure it overlaps slightly as this makes it easier to remove from the tin, then brush or spray with oil.

Put the pecans in a frying pan and toast for a few minutes until brown, then remove from the pan and set aside.

Put the butter and sugar in a mixing bowl and beat well until it begins to go pale and fluffy. Add the vanilla and 1 egg and beat well. Add all of the flour, salt, cinnamon, baking powder and the rest of the eggs and beat for 1 minute. Stir in the bananas and pecans and dollop the mixture into the prepared tin.

Bake in the oven for 55–60 minutes, or until a skewer inserted into the middle of the cake comes out clean.

Meanwhile, put the rum and sugar in a pan over a high heat, mix then boil furiously until it begins to get thicker, about 5 minutes. Set aside.

Once the cake is cooked, remove from the oven and pour over lots of the sugar syrup then sprinkle over some extra toasted pecans to decorate.

Serve with an ice cold daiquiri in a hammock under a palm tree.

'I just don't give a damn'
Chocolate Cake

No whisking, creaming or folding for this sponge, just throw it all in the bowl, mix like mad, then wait for the magic to happen in the oven. Thick, dark and lovely, it makes you want to just dive in with a spoon, with no friends invited. Serves 8 *(V)*

Vegetable oil, for oiling

140g (5oz) crème fraîche

130g (4½oz) very soft butter

230g (8¼oz) soft light brown sugar

Seeds of ½ vanilla pod or 2 drops of vanilla extract

4 eggs

180g (6½oz) plain flour

Pinch of salt

40g (1½oz) cocoa powder

10g (⅓oz) baking powder

Chocolate frosting

80g (1½oz) good dark chocolate (at least 64% cocoa solids)

130g (4½oz) butter, softened

Seeds of ½ vanilla pod or 2 drops of vanilla extract

250g (9oz) icing sugar

Equipment

Two x 20cm (8in) loose-bottomed sandwich tins

Preheat the oven to 180°C (350°F), Gas Mark 4. Oil the cake tins then line the bases with baking paper.

Put all the sponge ingredients in a large bowl and beat well for 2–3 minutes with an electric mixer or 3–4 minutes by hand until everything is combined. Dollop the mixture into the prepared cake tins, level the tops and bake for about 25–30 minutes, or until the cake is well risen and is coming away from the sides of the tin. The cake will be super, duper moist. Remove the cakes from the oven and leave to cool in the tins for about 5 minutes, then remove from the tins and cool on wire racks.

To make the frosting, put the chocolate in a heatproof bowl set over a pan of gently simmering water, making sure that the bottom of the bowl isn't touching the water, and leave to melt. Remove the bowl from the pan and set aside to cool slightly.

Put the butter, vanilla and icing sugar in a bowl and whisk together with an electric whisk until light and fluffy. Add the chocolate and beat until combined.

Once the cakes are cold, using a palette knife, spread one of the cakes with some of the frosting, then sandwich them both together and spread the rest of the frosting on the top.

Mojito Genoise

-The Genoise is a traditional Italian cake from Genoa, with a very light, buttery texture, and which uses no chemical raising agent. Needless to say, for this cake to work it needs the living daylights whisked out of it. Serves 8–10 *(V)*

Sugar syrup

150g (5oz) soft light brown sugar

40ml (1½fl oz) water

Finely grated zest and juice of 2 limes

80ml (3fl oz) white rum

Bunch of fresh mint, leaves only

Sponge

260g (9oz) caster sugar

6 eggs, lightly beaten

115g (4oz) butter, melted and cooled, plus extra for greasing

260g (9oz) plain flour

Buttercream

100g (3½oz) butter, softened

200g (7oz) icing sugar

Seeds of 1 vanilla pod or 2 drops of vanilla extract

Finely grated zest and juice of 1 lime, to taste

▼

Preheat the oven to 200°C (400°F), Gas Mark 6. Grease the cake tin and line the base with baking paper.

I make the sugar syrup first to allow the flavours to infuse. Put the sugar, water, lime juice and rum in a medium pan over a low heat. Cook until the sugar dissolves, then boil for 2–3 minutes until the syrup thickens. Add the mint and lime zest and set aside.

Fill a large saucepan around a third full of water. Place over a high heat and bring to the boil, then remove from the heat. Set a large heatproof bowl over the pan, making sure the base isn't touching the water. Add the sugar and eggs to the bowl and whisk. This causes them to foam up and gives a lighter, fluffier cake. The egg mixture should be whisked for about 10 minutes, then remove the bowl from the pan and continue to whisk for a further 5 minutes. The mixture is ready when it holds itself well in the bowl and, if you take a spoonful and then drop it back in, the resulting 'blob' should take 3–4 seconds to blend back into the mixture.

Once you have reached this 'ribbon stage', pour the melted butter into the bowl, around the sides (pouring it into the middle knocks out all the air). Fold the butter into the egg mix, moving the bowl around and scooping down to the bottom to fold the mixture over itself, using as few movements as possible to retain the air.

Next, add the flour and fold in until the mixture is uniform and smooth. Pour gently into the prepared tin and bake in the centre of the oven for about 30–35 minutes. When cooked, the sponge should spring back

▶

Mojito Genoise *(cont.)*

when pushed lightly, will be a light golden colour and a skewer inserted into the middle of the cake will come out clean. Leave to cool for 10 minutes or so, then remove from the tin and place on a wire rack to cool completely. Once it is cool, slice the cake in half horizontally and set aside.

To make the buttercream, put the butter, icing sugar and vanilla in a bowl and whisk until pale and fluffy. Add the lime zest and juice to taste.

To assemble the cake, put a dollop of buttercream on a serving plate (to stop the sponge sliding around the plate). Place the bottom of the sponge on the plate and brush with the reserved sugar syrup. Be quite liberal to make the cake really moist. Put a big dollop of buttercream on top and, using a palette knife, spread the buttercream over the cake until it is level. Take the top half of the cake, turn cut side up and brush with the sugar syrup. Turn it back over and put it on top of the buttercreamed sponge. Next, cover the whole cake with the buttercream, including the top and sides, making sure it is as smooth as possible with straight sides and top. Put the cake in the fridge for 10 minutes or so to firm up a little.

For the pecan coating, oil a baking tray. Put the sugar in a medium pan over a low heat and leave to melt, stirring as little as possible. If any sugar sticks to the sides of the pan, dip a pastry brush in water and brush it off. Once the sugar is melted bring the mixture to the boil and cook for 1 minute making sure it does not burn. Add the nuts and pour the mixture onto the prepared baking tray. Leave to cool. Once this has cooled right down, blitz the praline in an electric mixer or put it in plastic bag, smash it with a rolling pin and think of your boss.

Once the praline pieces are the size of breadcrumbs, use them to coat the sides of the cake.

This gateau makes a very different celebration cake for something special. Decorate with lime slices and whole pecans, if you like.

Orange & cardamom
Ricotta Cake

This is not a puffed-up, light-as-air, spongy cake, but a rich, moist, flattish cake enriched with crushed cardamom pods and best served as a dessert. Serves 8 (V)

180g (6½oz) butter, softened, plus extra for greasing

100g (3½oz) caster sugar, plus extra for sprinkling

100g (3½oz) soft light brown sugar

3 eggs, lightly beaten

200g (7oz) plain flour

1 egg yolk

1 heaped tsp baking powder

15–20 cardamom pods, seeds only, finely crushed

Finely grated zest of 4 medium oranges

1 tbsp orange blossom water (optional)

250g (9oz) ricotta cheese

Equipment

23cm (9in) springform cake tin

Preheat the oven to 180°C (350°F), Gas Mark 4. Grease the cake tin and sprinkle with sugar.

Put the butter and sugars in a large bowl and cream together until pale and fluffy. Add half of the eggs and half of the flour and beat well. Add the rest of the eggs, including the egg yolk, and flour together with the baking powder and beat well. Stir in the cardamom seeds, orange zest, orange blossom water, if using, and finally the ricotta cheese.

Dollop the mixture into the prepared cake tin and bake in the centre of the oven for 25–35 minutes. The cake will be firm on top but the crumb will still be very moist. Remove the cake from the oven and leave to cool in the tin before turning out and serving.

Best served fresh from the oven with a dollop of vanilla ice cream.

Strawberry & mascarpone
Swiss Roll

This is one deliriously decadent pud. A light vanilla sponge with Marsala strawberries and a potently rich mascarpone cream. There is no raising agent in this sponge delight, which instead relies entirely on your whisking powers for its leavening. Serves 6–8 (V)

Strawberry filling

250g (9oz) strawberries, hulled and sliced, plus a few sliced to decorate

2 tbsp granulated sugar

A splash of Marsala or orange juice

Sponge

3 eggs

80g (3oz) caster sugar, plus a bit extra for finishing

Seeds of ½ vanilla pod or 2 drops of vanilla extract

1 tbsp warm water

80g (3oz) plain flour

Pinch of salt

Mascarpone cream

250g (9oz) mascarpone

2 tbsp icing sugar

Seeds of ½ vanilla pod or 2 drops of vanilla extract

To make the filling, put about a third of the strawberries in a blender or food processor with the granulated sugar and blitz well. Transfer to a bowl and add the Marsala or orange juice. Stir in the remaining strawberries and place in the fridge. The flavour gets better the longer you leave it, so do this a few hours ahead if you can, though if you are ready to go now then a minimum of 30 minutes is fine.

Preheat the oven to 190°C (375°F), Gas Mark 5. Grease the Swiss roll tin and line the base with baking paper.

For the sponge, put the eggs, sugar and vanilla in large bowl and beat with an electric whisk until the mixture is very pale yellow, foamy and mousse-like. Fold in the warm water with a large metal spoon. This helps prevent the Swiss roll from cracking when you roll it later. Sift over the flour and salt and fold in gently with the metal spoon. Don't overmix here or you will knock out the air and the Swiss roll will lose its sponginess. The trick is to incorporate all the flour with as few 'folds' as possible.

Pour the mixture into the prepared tin and level it gently with a palette knife or the back of a large spoon. Bake in the oven for 10–15 minutes, or until it has shrunk a little from the sides of the tin and feels springy to the touch. Remove from the oven and turn the cake out onto a sheet of baking paper sprinkled with caster sugar. Leave for 10 minutes, then gently peel the lining paper off the sponge and leave to cool completely.

▶

Equipment

23 x 33cm (9 x 13in) Swiss roll tin or small roasting tin lined with baking paper

In a large bowl, gently mix together all the ingredients for the mascarpone cream until smooth.

To assemble the cake, trim off any rough edges of the sponge with a sharp serrated knife if necessary to get the sides nice and tidy, then spread the mascarpone cream all over the sponge, leaving a small margin so it does not squelch out when it is rolled. Spoon the macerated strawberries out of the purée and scatter over the mascarpone filling. Drizzle a third of the strawberry purée over it as well (reserving the rest).

Here comes the best bit. With the shortest side facing you, begin to roll up the sponge (away from you) using the baking paper to help. Try to do it as tightly as you can for an impressive-looking finish. Once you have rolled it all up, make sure the join is underneath so it does not come undone. Carefully lift onto a serving plate. You can do this with your hands or use two fish slices or spatulas.

Sprinkle with some caster sugar and decorate with extra sliced strawberries. Serve in slices with the remaining strawberry sauce drizzled over. Best on a hot summer's day with some fresh lemonade.

Battenberg

I once punked this up for a birthday party – the yellow sponge became black and the pink became a psychedelic shocking pink. A year on, I'm still trying to get the black dye off the kitchen surfaces, but the cake was a great success. Serves 6–8 (V)

100g (3½oz) apricot jam

150g (5oz) cold butter, cubed

150g (5oz) caster sugar, plus extra for sprinkling

150g (5oz) plain flour

1 heaped tsp baking powder

Pinch of salt

3 medium eggs

Few drops of both yellow and pink (or red) food colouring

Icing sugar, for dusting

250g (9oz) golden marzipan

Equipment

Two 22 x 12cm (8¾ x 4¾in) loaf tins

Preheat the oven to 180°C (350°F), Gas Mark 4. Line the loaf tins with baking paper. The mixture only came up a third of the way in each, which worked well.

Put the jam in a small pan and heat gently until warm then remove the pan from the heat and leave to cool.

Put the butter, sugar, flour, baking powder and salt in an electric mixer and mix until the mixture resembles breadcrumbs. Add the eggs, one at a time, beating well after each addition. If you are doing this by hand, cream the butter and sugar together in a bowl, add the eggs, beating well after each addition, then add the flour, baking powder and salt and stir to combine.

Divide the mixture into 2 bowls and colour one with the yellow colouring and the other with the pink. You don't need much pink or red colouring, usually only one drop, or you'll end up with a psychedelic battenburg!

Dollop the yellow cake mixture into one tin and the pink into the other and bake in the oven for 20–25 minutes, or until a skewer inserted into the thickest part comes out clean.

Leave the sponges to cool for 10 minutes. Place some baking paper sprinkled with sugar on a wire rack and turn the sponges out onto them. This will give the sponges a more even top. Leave to cool completely.

▶

Battenberg *(cont.)*

Once the sponges are cold, peel off the baking paper and with the longest side facing you, cut the sponges in half horizontally, Stick the pieces together with the apricot jam as in the picture.

Dust the work surface with some icing sugar, place the marzipan on the sugar and knead slightly to soften. Roll the marzipan out to a rectangle that is large enough to cover the longest edges of the cake. Place the sponge on the marzipan to measure so you have enough marzipan to wrap around the cake.

To assemble the cake, spread some jam over one side of the cake and place it spread side down at the edge of your rectangle. Then spread all of the remaining 3 long sides with the jam. Roll the cake along the marzipan, pressing gently as you go to make sure it sticks well.

Smooth the cake over with the palm of your hand and leave to harden for 15 minutes. Quite possibly my favourite cake, I would never try and compete with Mr K but this cake is very very close to it!

Gluten-free Irish cream
Coffee Cake

Eaten too much bread recently and wheat giving you gip? Try this gluten-free cake for a bloat-free bite. Serves 8–10 (V)

200g (7oz) soft light brown sugar

Pinch of salt

200g (7oz) cold butter, cut into cubes, plus extra for greasing

200g (7oz) gluten-free self-raising flour, plus 1 tsp baking powder

4 eggs, lightly beaten

Seeds of ½ vanilla pod or 2 drops of vanilla extract

80ml (3fl oz) very strong black coffee or 4–5 tbsp coffee essence

Small handful of instant coffee granules, to sprinkle

Irish cream buttercream

125g (4½oz) butter, softened

250g (9oz) icing sugar

Seeds of ½ vanilla pod or 2 drops of vanilla extract

2 tbsp of Irish cream liqueur, or to taste

Equipment

Two x 20cm (8in) loose-bottomed sandwich tins

Preheat the oven to 180°C (350°F), Gas Mark 4. Grease the cake tins and line the bases with baking paper.

Put the brown sugar, salt, butter, flour and baking powder into an electric mixer fitted with a paddle and mix briefly until it looks like breadcrumbs. Don't overmix, or it will go into a big sticky lump. If you don't have a mixer, then either blitz in a food processor or put the ingredients into a large bowl and, using your thumb and fingers, rub the mixture together until it resembles breadcrumbs.

Gradually add the eggs in three lots, beating well after each addition, then add the vanilla and coffee and beat hard for 2–3 minutes.

Divide the mixture evenly between the prepared tins and bake for about 30 minutes, but check them after 25 minutes. The cakes are ready when they have shrunk slightly from the sides of the tin, the tops spring back when pressed gently and a skewer inserted into the thickest part comes out clean. Once the cakes are cooked, leave them to cool in the tins.

Meanwhile, make the buttercream. Put the butter, icing sugar and vanilla in a bowl and beat until it is light and fluffy. Stir in the Irish cream liqueur and mix to combine. Set aside.

Once the cakes are cold, remove them from the tins and peel off the baking paper. Spread half the buttercream over one sponge and put the other sponge on top. Spread the top layer with buttercream then sprinkle over some coffee granules. The coffee granules will dissolve after 30 minutes or so. Serve with tea or coffee.

Rich boozy
Fruit Cake

This is ideal for Christmas. Make a month before and 'feed' with liquor regularly, though I normally find myself making it late on 23rd December with drunken friends singing carols in the next room. With or without the alcoholic feed-a-thon, this cake is a winner.
Serves 16–18 *(V)*

400g (14oz) currants, sultanas and raisins

100g (3½oz) dried cranberries

100g (3½oz) Medjool dates, deseeded and roughly chopped

100g (3½oz) ready-to-eat dried apricots, roughly chopped

80g (3oz) mixed peel

500ml (18fl oz) brandy or a good Jamaican rum or builder's tea

250g (9oz) butter

250g (9oz) muscovado sugar

5 eggs, lightly beaten

250g (9oz) plain flour, plus 80g (3oz) for tossing

▼

Put the currants, sultanas, raisins, cranberries, dates, apricots and mixed peel in a bowl, cover with the brandy, rum or tea and leave to steep overnight.

The next day, preheat the oven to 180°C (350°F), Gas Mark 4. Grease the tin and line the base and sides with a double thickness of baking paper. Put a double thickness of paper around the outside of the tin too. The cake needs a long cooking time so the paper will protect the outside from cooking too quickly.

Put the butter and sugar in a large bowl and cream together until it begins to go a little paler and more fluffy. Add half of the eggs and half the 250g (9oz) flour and stir to just combine, then add the rest of the eggs, flour, baking powder, mixed spice, nutmeg and ground ginger and mix to just combine. Finally, drain the fruit, reserving the brandy, rum or tea, and toss the fruit in the 80g (3oz) of flour. This will stop the fruit from sinking to the bottom of the cake during baking. Add the fruit together with the treacle, hazelnuts, lime zest, orange zest and ginger and stir until the mixture looks uniform.

▶

15g (½oz) baking powder

2 tsp mixed spice

1 tsp ground nutmeg

1 tbsp ground ginger

1 tbsp treacle

100g (3½oz) hazelnuts, chopped

Finely grated zest of 3 limes

Finely grated zest of 1 orange

2 x 2cm (¾in) pieces fresh ginger, peeled and grated

Equipment

23cm (9in) deep round baking tin

Dollop the mixture into the prepared cake tin and make a well in the centre. This will ensure the cake does not rise into a peak and cooks with a level top. Bake in the oven for 1 hour, covering the top loosely with foil if necessary to prevent it becoming too dark, then reduce the oven temperature to 150°C (300°F), Gas Mark 2 and cook for a further 1½ hours or until a skewer inserted into the centre comes out clean and the cake has shrunken slightly from the sides of the tin.

Once the cake is cooked, remove from the oven and prick holes over the top. Pour some of the reserved liquid over the top of the cake so it runs into the holes and 'feeds' the cake with booziness. Leave the cake to cool in the tin. It can be eaten straight away or wrapped up in paper and foil for up to a month and fed once a week with the alcohol.

If you want to decorate the cake as a Christmas cake, you can cover it with marzipan and sugar paste, which should be done a day or so before you intend to eat it. Or you could tie a ribbon round it, put rows of dried fruit and nuts on top and glaze with warm apricot jam.

'I can't believe you made that'
Cake

This cake is made with chocolate cigarillos, which can be bought easily on the internet, but should you need to make the cake today, use chocolate fingers, chocolate flake bars, or even matchmakers around the edge. Serves 10–12 (V)

Vegetable oil or oil spray

200g (7oz) butter, softened

200g (7oz) caster sugar

4 eggs

140g (5oz) plain flour

60g (2½oz) cocoa powder

Pinch of salt

2 tsp baking powder

400g (14oz) plain, milk, or white chocolate cigarillos (about 75–80 in total)

Buttercream

250g (9oz) butter, softened

500g (1lb 2oz) icing sugar

100g (3½oz) good dark chocolate (at least 70% cocoa solids), melted and slightly cooled

Decoration (optional)

Fresh flowers, for a Christening cake

Strawberries or raspberries, for the girls

Figs, quartered, for the boys

Equipment

20cm (8in) round deep cake tin

Preheat the oven to 180°C (350°F), Gas Mark 4. Line the cake tin with baking paper and brush or spray with oil.

Cream together the butter and sugar in a large bowl until they begin to go pale. Add half the eggs and half the flour and mix well. Add the rest of the eggs, flour, cocoa powder, salt and baking powder and beat for a minute or two until the mixture is uniform. Dollop into the prepared tin and bake in the oven for about 30–40 minutes, or until a skewer inserted in the middle comes out clean. Leave to cool in the tin.

Meanwhile, make the buttercream. Put the butter and icing sugar in a bowl and whisk together until the mixture begins to go fluffy. Add the cooled melted chocolate and whisk for a further 2 minutes.

Once the cake is completely cool, remove from the tin. Carefully cut the top flat with a large serrated knife. (Eat this bit as a chef's perk.) Turn the cake upside down on a 20cm (8in) cake board so that the bottom now becomes a nice flat top. Split the cake horizontally and sandwich the top and bottom together with a 1cm (½in) layer of buttercream. Spread half the remaining buttercream all over the top and sides of the cake, making it as smooth as possible. Put it in the fridge to set before doing another layer. This makes it much easier to get good squared-off edges.

Gently push the cigarillos vertically onto the sides of the cake, positioning them as straight as possible and making sure they touch the bottom. The next step is up to you. I can't tell you the wide-eyed looks you'll get when you walk into the room holding the finished cake. Decorate with fresh flowers for a Christening or wedding, strawberries for a big family gathering or with figs for a man's birthday. Serve with a self-satisfied grin.

Victoria Sandwich

Victorious Victoria Sandwich, the original sponge cake, and still the best. Serves 8–10 (V)

200g (7oz) butter, softened, plus extra for greasing

200g (7oz) caster sugar

4 eggs

Seeds of ½ vanilla pod or 2 drops of vanilla extract

200g (7oz) plain flour

2 tsp baking powder

1–2 tbsp warm water, if required

Filling

5–6 tbsp good strawberry jam

300ml (11fl oz) double cream

30g (1¼oz) icing sugar, plus extra for sprinkling

Seeds of ½ vanilla pod or 2 drops of vanilla extract

Equipment

Two x 20cm (8in) loose-bottomed sandwich tins

Preheat the oven to 180°C (350°F), Gas Mark 4. Grease the cake tins and line the bases with baking paper.

Put the butter and caster sugar in a bowl and beat together well. Add 2 eggs, the vanilla and half the flour and beat well. Add the other 2 eggs, the rest of the flour and the baking powder and beat. If the mixture is stiff add the warm water.

Divide the mixture between the prepared tins and level the tops with the back of a spoon. Bake in the oven for 30 minutes, or until the sides of the sponge have shrunk slightly from the side of the tin, the sponge springs back slightly when pressed and a skewer inserted into the middle comes out clean. Leave the sponges to cool in the tin.

Once the sponges are completely cool, remove them from the tin and place on a serving dish. Spread one sponge with the jam.

Put the cream, icing sugar and vanilla in a large bowl and whip until thick. Dollop the whipped cream mixture on top of the jam, then put the other sponge on top and sprinkle with some icing sugar.

Serve with a very hot cup of Earl Grey tea and some cucumber sandwiches (crusts removed).

Three-tier
Red Velvet Cake

Celebrations should be marked with beautiful, memorable cakes. This favourite of mine looks impressive, but is actually quite simple. Each tier uses the same ingredients in different quantities, so the chart will help if you want to make fewer tiers. Use a good brand of red colouring and, for a strong, vibrant colour, avoid 'natural red'. Ready-to-roll sugarpaste or fondant icing is available from supermarkets or specialist cake shops.

	Small Tier	Medium Tier	Large Tier
Round cake tin	15cm (6in)	23cm (9in)	30cm (12in)
Butter, softened	150g (5oz)	350g (12oz)	650g (1lb 7oz)
Castor sugar	150g (5oz)	350g (12oz)	650g (1lb 7oz)
Eggs	2	6	10
Vanilla essence	a few drops	½ tsp	1 tbsp
Salt	small pinch	small pinch	large pinch
Plain flour	125g (4½oz)	300g (10oz)	575g (1lb 5oz)
Cocoa powder	25g (1oz)	50g (2oz)	75g (3oz)
Baking powder	7g (¼oz)	15g (½oz)	35g (1¼oz)
Red colouring	1 tbsp	50ml (2fl oz)	100ml (3½fl oz)
Baking time	40–45mins	1hr 15mins	1hr 25–1hr 30mins
Sugarpaste	450g (1lb)	800g (1¾lb)	1.25kg (2¾lb)
Cake board	15cm (6in)	23cm (9in)	30cm (12in)
For the buttercream			
Butter, softened	80g (3oz)	250g (9oz)	400g (14oz)
Icing sugar	200g (7oz)	600g (1lb 5oz)	1kg (2lb 2oz)
Cream cheese	25g (1oz)	75g (3oz)	120g (4½oz)

Lining the tins

Take your first cake tin and draw round it twice onto baking paper. Cut out both circles. Measure the circumference of the tin with string, then cut a long strip of paper the length of the string and fold in half lengthways. Grease the tin with melted butter and place one of the paper circles into the base. Grease, add a second circle, and grease again. Press the paper strip onto the inside edge of the tin and grease. If you're making multiple tiers, repeat with the other tins.

Baking the cakes

Preheat the oven to 180°C (350°F), Gas Mark 4. Put the butter and sugar into a large bowl and beat together until light and fluffy. Gradually beat in the eggs, vanilla and salt, and half of the flour to prevent the mixture from curdling. Add the remaining flour, cocoa powder and baking powder and give it a final beat to mix together. Add the food colouring and mix well. Spoon into the prepared tin and bake for the recommended time. The cake is ready when firm to the touch and a skewer inserted into the centre comes out clean. Leave to cool in the tin for 5 minutes before turning out onto a wire rack (you may need two racks side by side for the largest cake). Peel off the lining paper and leave to cool.

Making the buttercream

Prepare the ingredients for the relevant number of tiers. You can make the buttercream in a single batch so you'll only need one large bowl. Cream together the softened butter and icing sugar until light and fluffy. Beat in the cream cheese and a few drops of vanilla essence to taste. Cover the surface of the buttercream with clingfilm and chill until ready to use.

Cutting and layering the cakes

Using a long-bladed serrated knife, carefully cut the smallest cake in half and sandwich back together with 3 heaped tablespoons of buttercream. Spread a teaspoon of buttercream onto the centre of the smallest cake board and put the cake on top (this will stop the cake sliding off the board). Cut the remaining cakes in the same way, using 6 heaped tablespoons of buttercream to sandwich the medium cake and 8 heaped tablespoons of buttercream for the large one. Place the medium cake upside down on its cake board and the large cake on the largest cake board. Spread half the remaining buttercream in a thin layer over the top and sides of the cakes to cover. Refrigerate until set to the touch and then spread the remaining buttercream over the cakes to give a perfect finish.

▶

Covering with sugarpaste

Cut a piece of string for each cake to measure the combined length of the top and sides – this will be the size to which to roll your circle of sugarpaste. Ice just one cake at a time, as sugarpaste can dry out very quickly. Make sure your work surface is clean and dry, then knead the sugarpaste until warm and pliable. Place 2 tablespoons of icing sugar in a small sieve and use to lightly dust your work surface. Roll out the sugarpaste to 3–4mm (⅛in) thick and keep turning so that it stays circular. Carefully slide your hands and arms under the sugarpaste, lift centrally over the cake and lay onto the buttercream (you could use a large rolling pin for this instead – simply hold the pin over the centre of the sugarpaste and flip the paste over it. Lift, position, and roll over the cake). Dust your hands with a little icing sugar and rub them gently over the cake to make sure the sugarpaste has stuck to the buttercream underneath. Use a sharp long-bladed knife to trim the edges, cutting downwards cleanly (keep wiping the knife blade, else paste will build up and make it difficult to get a clean cut). Repeat with the remaining cakes and sugarpaste. Save any trimmings to make decorations, flowers or frills – keep well wrapped in clingfilm until ready to use, to prevent from drying out.

Stacking the cakes

To stack the cakes, you'll need the help of some dowelling rods, because the sponge and icing are too soft to support the weight of each other. Dowels can be bought from specialist cake shops; however, as every cake is different they do need to be cut to size. Only the bottom two tiers need them, so you will need eight rods in total. Hold a rod at the side of the cake and mark with a pencil where the icing comes to. Cut the rod and three others to the same length. Push the rods into the cake about 5cm (2in) away from the sides, to form the four corners of a square in the centre of the cake. They should not rise above the level of the icing. If you have miscalculated and the dowelling is too long, remove it and shave off any excess with a sharp knife. Measure, cut and insert the rods in the same way for the medium cake. The three cakes can now be stacked directly on to each other. Once they're stacked, it's best not to move them about, so it's safest to assemble them at your venue or in the position you want them to be displayed.

Serve with Bride and Groom and lots of alcohol!

Hazelnut & lemon
Madeleines

There is many an argument over the origin of these scallop-shaped cakes. They have been linked to Polish and French royalty, with the exiled Duke of Lorraine thrown in for good measure. Proust spoke of these plump little cakes in his book *Remembrance of Things Past*. For authenticity, they should be made in a Madeleine mould, which, of course, is readily available to buy on the internet. Makes 14 *(V)*

Vegetable oil or oil spray, for oiling

4 eggs

100g (3½oz) caster sugar

80g (3oz) butter, melted

Seeds of ½ vanilla pod or 2 drops of vanilla extract

Pinch of salt

100g (3½oz) plain flour

40g (1½oz) toasted hazelnuts (see page 44) – finely chopped or ground almonds also work

Finely grated zest of 1 lemon

Equipment

1 large Madeleine tin

1 piping bag fitted with medium round nozzle

Preheat the oven to 180°C (350°F), Gas Mark 4. Oil the Madeleine tin.

Put the eggs in a large bowl and whisk until they have almost doubled in volume, then while still whisking gradually add the sugar down the sides of the bowl. This will take about 10–15 minutes with an electric mixer and the mixture will be very light, fluffy and mousse-like.

Add the melted butter around the sides of the bowl so as not to knock out all the air, then add the vanilla and fold the mixture over itself to combine, using as few strokes as possible so as not to knock out the air. Sift the salt and half the flour over the mixture and carefully fold it into the batter. Once this is combined, sift the other half in and repeat.

Scatter over the nuts and lemon zest and stir to combine. Pour the mixture into the piping bag and pipe the mixture into the prepared Madeleine moulds, filling them two-thirds full. Bake in the oven for about 10 minutes, or until the Madeleines are springy to the touch and are turning a light golden brown colour.

Serve straight from the oven as a petit-four with tea or coffee.

Cupcakes

In theory, simple sponge cakes dressed with a mountain of soft creamy icing should not be the object of such media obsession. Neither should they inspire debate or provoke competition... And yet, cupcakes do exactly this! Now firmly embedded in our national psyche, cupcakes have become an integral part of an afternoon tea. They are easy to make, and a joy to decorate during family baking sessions. *Makes 12 cupcakes (V)*

200g (7oz) butter, softened

200g (7oz) caster sugar

1 tsp vanilla extract

4 eggs

200g (7oz) plain flour

Pinch of salt

2 tsp baking powder

2 tsp milk or a splash of water (optional)

Sprinkles, sparkles or shaved chocolate, to decorate

Vanilla syrup

200ml (7fl oz) water

100g (3½oz) granulated sugar

1 vanilla pod

Preheat the oven to 160°C (315°F), Gas mark 2–3. Line the muffin tin with 12 paper cases.

Put the butter and caster sugar in a large bowl and cream together until light and fluffy. Add the vanilla, then the eggs, one at a time, beating well after each addition. If the mixture begins to look curdled, add a tablespoon of the flour and beat well until smooth.

Once the eggs have all been beaten in, add the flour, salt and baking powder and mix together until just combined. If the mixture is a bit stiff, add the 2 teaspoons of milk or a splash of water to loosen it a little.

Using an ice-cream scoop, plop the mixture into the paper cases and bake in the oven for 25–30 minutes, or until the cakes spring back slightly when pressed, they have that 'freshly baked cake' smell and when a skewer inserted into the middle comes out clean.

While the cakes are baking, make the vanilla syrup. Put all the ingredients into a pan over a low heat and stir gently until the sugar has

▼   ▶

Buttercream

300g (10½oz) butter, softened

750g (1lb 11oz) icing sugar

Seeds of 1–1½ vanilla pods

Yellow, blue and red food colouring (optional)

Equipment

12-hole muffin tin

Piping bag fitted with a 1cm star nozzle or a 1cm straight nozzle (optional)

dissolved. Turn up the heat and boil for 1 minute, then take the pan off the heat.

As soon as the cakes come out of the oven, brush them liberally with the vanilla syrup to make them really nice and moist. Leave the cakes to cool.

Meanwhile, make the buttercream. Put all the ingredients, except the food colouring, in a bowl and beat well until the mixture becomes light and fluffy. You can colour the buttercream with a couple of drops of food colouring, if you like. Set aside until needed.

Once the cupcakes are completely cool, you can ice them. Do this either with a palette knife, or use a piping bag fitted with a 1cm star nozzle or a 1cm straight nozzle. Put the buttercream into the piping bag and squeeze onto the cakes, or smooth on with the palette knife, then decorate with your choice of sprinkles and sparkles or pieces of shaved chocolate.

Savoury Baking

With all the exacting standards demanded by cakes, desserts and other patisserie items, it's nice to get stuck into simpler cooking with a good bit of meat, veg or fish. Less precious than the sweeter dishes, and much more forgiving should the ingredients or method not be adhered to 100%, these savoury recipes are predominantly comfort-food dishes, meals you'll want to curl up with, and food that makes everything feel just that little bit better.

'As a child my family's menu consisted of two choices: take it or leave it.'

Buddy Hackett
Comedian and Actor
1924 – 2003

Camembert
& roasted garlic

If you have a hot date or an important business meeting later on, this dish is best avoided. If, however, your calendar is free for the rest of the day, then Camembert and roasted garlic is a most pleasurable snack. Serves 2 *(V if veggie cheese is used)*

2 bulbs of garlic, unpeeled with the tops sliced off

40g (1½oz) butter

80ml (3fl oz) extra-virgin olive oil

Salt and freshly ground black pepper

1 squidge of honey

2 fresh rosemary sprigs

3 bay leaves

200–250g (7–9oz) Camembert, plastic wrapping and lid removed but still in its wooden box, at room temperature

1 French baguette, ripped into 10cm (4in) pieces and sliced horizontally

Preheat the oven to 200°C (400°F), Gas Mark 6.

Place the garlic cut side down in a large roasting tin. Add the butter, oil, a pinch of salt, a couple of twists of black pepper, the honey, rosemary and bay leaves and bake in the oven for 40–45 minutes. After 30–35 minutes put a large cross in the top of the Camembert and add it to the oven. Make sure the plastic covering and lid is removed, but it is still in its cardboard box. Add the French baguette to warm up too.

Once the garlic is soft, the bread is extra crunchy and the cheese is all soft and gooey, remove from the oven.

Serve everything on a big sharing plate. Break off a piece of crusty bread, squeeze out the tender flesh of the garlic along with a healthy dose of cheese and smear it liberally over the bread.

Serve with a chutney or relish and a good glass of red wine.

Butternut Squash

with quinoa, feta, basil & mint

Quinoa is pronounced Keen-wa and looks a bit like couscous, though it is much healthier as it is a complete protein. This dish is for those 'there's a vegetarian coming for dinner' evenings. So tasty, all the carnivores will want a piece of it. Serves 4 (V)

2 large butternut squash, halved lengthways and deseeded

Drizzle of extra-virgin olive oil

Salt and freshly ground black pepper

1 bulb of garlic, unpeeled with the top sliced off

310g (11oz) quinoa

2 red peppers, sliced into strips

1 large pinch of fennel seeds

2 handfuls of pine nuts, toasted (see page 44)

1 small red chilli, deseeded and finely diced

400g (14oz) feta cheese, crumbled into largish chunks

1 large squeeze of honey

1 bunch of fresh basil

1 bunch of fresh mint

Preheat the oven to 200°C (400°F), Gas Mark 6.

Place the squash cut side up on a large shallow baking tray and drizzle with the oil, then season with a pinch of salt and a twist of black pepper. Put the garlic on the tray next to the squash and bake in the oven for 30 minutes.

Meanwhile, make the quinoa according to the packet instructions then remove the pan from the heat and leave to cool in the pan.

Remove the squash from the oven and sprinkle the red peppers over the tray (not on the squash). Sprinkle the fennel seeds over the squash, then remove the garlic from the tray and set aside. Next, put the squash back in the oven and bake for 30 minutes, or until the squash is soft when tested with a spoon.

Add the pine nuts, chilli, feta, red peppers and honey to the quinoa. Squeeze the garlic flesh from the skins and stir everything together. Season to taste with salt and pepper. Place the squash on individual serving plates and divide the quinoa mix among the squashes. I spread it all over leaving a border of 1cm (½in) and pile it up high for dramatic effect.

Tear up the basil and mint leaves and scatter over the top. Serve immediately.

Omelette
Arnold Bennett

A big, fat, fluffy omelette that is made like giant soufflé. I rarely buy fresh truffles, but when I do this is my favourite dish in which to put them. At other times, I use truffle-infused oil, which you can buy from most good Italian delis. Serves 4

40g (1½oz) butter, plus a small blob of butter

100g (3½oz) mixed mushrooms, such as chestnut, cep and button, sliced then roughly chopped

1 tbsp sherry (wine will do just fine instead)

150ml (5fl oz) milk

150ml (5fl oz) double cream

40g (1½oz) plain flour

Pinch of freshly grated nutmeg

Pinch of mustard powder

Salt and freshly ground black pepper

5 eggs, separated

Handful of fresh chives, finely chopped

Squeeze of lemon juice

Fresh truffles or truffle oil

Equipment

Large ovenproof sauté pan or deepish ovenproof frying pan, or you can use a 20cm (8in) sandwich tin

Preheat the oven to 220°C (425°F), Gas Mark 7.

Put the small blob of butter in a small pan over a medium–high heat and cook until the butter starts to sizzle. Add the mushrooms, turn up the heat and cook for 1 minute. Carefully tip in the sherry – it may flame for a second, if so keep shaking the pan until the flames die down. Remove the pan from the heat. Put a sieve over a measuring jug and pour the mushroom mix into the sieve. Set the mushrooms aside and add enough milk and cream to the cooking liquor to make 300ml (11fl oz).

Put the 40g (1½oz) of butter in the same pan used to cook the mushrooms and melt over a medium heat. Add the flour, nutmeg and mustard, stir well and cook for a minute or two. Remove the pan from the heat and gradually add the mushroom and cream liquid, beating hard between each addition with a wooden spoon. Adding it too quickly means the mixture may go lumpy. If this happens whisk furiously for a few minutes to get rid of any unsightly lumps!

Return the pan to the heat, cook the mixture until it thickens, then season with salt and pepper and beat hard for a minute. As this mixture is going to be 'diluted' with the eggs, make the seasoning stronger than usual.

Add the egg yolks, one by one, stirring well after each addition. Remove the pan from the heat, add the mushrooms and chives then set aside.

Put the egg whites and a squeeze of lemon juice into a large bowl and whisk until stiff. Put a spoonful of the egg white mix in with the mushroom mixture and stir. This will loosen the mushroom mixture and make it easier to stir into the egg whites. Then pour the mushroom mixture into the egg whites. Pour it down the side of the whites rather than in the middle so you do not knock out all of the air which has been incorporated into it. Slowly fold this together and then carefully spoon into a large, greased, ovenproof sauté pan, frying pan or cake tin. If using the cake tin, put on a baking tray. Bake in the oven for about 8 minutes, or until the omelette is risen and a light golden brown. Remove from the oven, shave some truffles over the top or drizzle with a little truffle oil and serve immediately.

Serve on a Sunday while reading the papers with the TV humming comfortingly in the background – divine pillowy mushroomness. Best eaten with a crisp rocket salad.

Crème fraîche
Quiche Lorraine

Using crème fraîche instead of milk and cream gives a superior taste to this Alsacienne favourite. Make it a day in advance and let the flavours develop for full impact.

Serves 8–10

1 quantity of savoury shortcrust pastry (see page 220) or 500g (1lb 2oz) shop-bought shortcrust pastry

1 2 tbsp olive oil

1 medium onion, peeled and finely diced

5 rashers of streaky bacon, diced

430g (15oz) crème fraîche

4 eggs, lightly beaten

Freshly ground black pepper

Equipment

23cm (9in) fluted flan dish, about 3.5cm (1¾in) deep

Preheat the oven to 190°C (375°F), Gas Mark 5.

If using homemade pastry, make it according to the recipe on page 220. Line the flan dish with the pastry (see page 113) and 'blind bake' (see page 113) for 20 minutes. Remove the baking beans and paper from the pastry case, then return to the oven and bake for a further 10 minutes. Remove from the oven and set aside. Turn the oven down to 150°C (300°F), Gas Mark 2.

The filling can be prepared while the pastry is baking. Heat the oil in a frying pan over a low heat, add the onion and fry until soft and translucent with no colour. This can take a good 15 minutes. If the onion looks as if it is drying out, just add a splash more oil or water.

Remove the onion from the pan and set aside. Add the bacon to the pan, turn up the heat slightly and cook for 5–6 minutes. Remove from the heat and add half of the bacon to the base of the flan dish. Place the flan dish on a flat baking tray.

Whisk the crème fraîche and the eggs together gently in a large bowl, then season with pepper. Stir in the onions. You will not need any salt as the bacon is already very salty. Pour the mixture into the flan dish all the way to the top. Sprinkle the remaining bacon on top of the quiche and bake in the oven for 35–40 minutes, or until the filling no longer wobbles.

Good to eat hot but best eaten cold, giving the mixture a chance to settle. Kept in the fridge it tastes even better the next day. Perfect with salad, cold meats and a very chilled white wine.

Totally lazy
Mini Sausage Rolls

I make these often – sometimes the sausage shoots rather rudely out of its skin, sometimes it doesn't. To guarantee your sausage does not escape its roll during cooking, the sausage 'skin' can be slipped off before encasing it in pastry. Makes 16 rolls

1 quantity of puff pastry (see page 218) or 500g (1lb 2oz) shop-bought puff pastry

Plain flour, for dusting

1 egg, beaten

8 herby sausages (the best you can afford), cut in two

Salt and freshly ground black pepper

Small handful of thyme leaves

Preheat the oven to 200°C (400°F), Gas Mark 6.

If making homemade pastry, make it according to the recipe on page 218. Roll the pastry out on a floured surface to a rectangle of about 48 x 32cm (19 x 12½in) and bash the pastry with the rolling pin a bit. Puff pastry is made of fine layers and normally you have to be very delicate with it. For sausage rolls the pastry needs to be slightly puffed but not too much, so bashing it with a rolling pin reduces the amount it puffs up.

Cut the large rectangle in half lengthways, then cut both smaller rectangles into eight equal sections. You now have 16 rectangles in total. Brush one end of each rectangle with a little of the beaten egg, lay a piece of sausage at the other end, then season the sausage with salt and pepper and sprinkle with thyme leaves. Roll the sausage up in the pastry to enclose and repeat with all the sausages. For a flavour variation add sage, parsley or chopped rosemary. Put the sausage rolls in the fridge for 20 minutes for the pastry to harden.

Once the pastry is hard, remove them from the fridge and score the tops with a sharp knife for decoration or prick with a fork. Brush well all over with the rest of the beaten egg and bake in the oven for 25–30 minutes, or until the pastry has turned a golden brown and looks crisp. Remove from the oven and leave to cool slightly before serving.

Glam
Mac & Cheese

A classic 'just for the family' dish turned completely on its head. Serve this little number in individual portions to make it worthy of any dinner-party table. I have used Dolcelatte as my cheese of choice. It is softer round the edges than Stilton and incredibly moreish. It dresses up this British classic to make it a meal fit for royalty. Serves 4 glamorous guests

340g (12oz) macaroni

Salt and freshly ground black pepper

80g (3oz) pancetta, diced

1 small handful of fresh thyme leaves

3 spring onions, trimmed and finely sliced

100g (3½oz) breadcrumbs

1 handful of chopped fresh parsley

Cheese sauce

40g (1½oz) butter

40g (1½oz) plain flour

Pinch of ground nutmeg

1 tsp mustard powder

200ml (7fl oz) milk

285ml (10fl oz) double cream

200g (7oz) dolcelatte or Gorgonzola cheese (if you are not a blue cheese fan a good British Cheddar will also suit instead)

115g (4oz) Parmesan cheese

▼

Preheat the oven to 200°C (400°F), Gas Mark 6.

Cook the macaroni in a large pan of boiling salted water. It needs to be cooked to just under what you would normally do as the pasta will be cooked again in the oven. Drain, return to the pan and set aside.

Fry the pancetta in a medium frying pan over a gentle heat until it just starts to brown and crisp up, then add the thyme leaves and spring onions and cook for a further 3 minutes. Remove the pan from the heat and add its contents to the pasta.

For the sauce, put the butter, flour, nutmeg and mustard in a small pan set over a medium heat and cook until the butter has melted. Mix the milk and cream together in a jug and add a little to the flour and butter in the pan, stirring well. Keep adding the milk mixture, bit by bit, stirring well each time. This will prevent the sauce from going lumpy. The temptation is to put all the milk in at once only to find you are left with clumps of

▶

Equipment

Large shallow casserole dish or 4 large ramekins

flour floating on the surface. Should this happen, take the pan off the heat and whisk it like crazy. This normally does the trick to eliminate all the lumps! Make sure you get the spoon into the 'corners' of the pan as stray mounds of flour often lurk there. Once the sauce has fully come together, turn up the heat and boil for a minute or two. The sauce will thicken considerably, then remove the pan from the heat. Add two-thirds of both of the cheeses to the sauce while it is still hot and combine well. It may be a bit lumpy but that is fine. Season to taste with salt and pepper and add to the pasta mix. Stir everything together and spoon into a shallow casserole dish or 4 individual large ramekins.

Sprinkle the top with the rest of the cheese and the breadcrumbs and bake in the oven for about 20 minutes, or until the cheese starts to bubble and the topping goes crumbly and brown. Sprinkle with chopped parsley and serve while hot.

Pork Pies
with cider

Some like the jelly, others really don't. These pies are aspic-free and wrapped in the easiest pastry you can make. When it comes to peeling hard-boiled eggs, remember that older eggs peel more easily, so try to buy them in advance. But if your eggs are fresh, add a pinch of baking soda to the water, which also makes them easier to peel.
Makes 8 individual pies

Hot water crust pastry

430g (15oz) plain flour, plus extra for dusting

½ tsp salt

Few twists of black pepper

1 egg yolk

80g (3oz) butter

100g (3½oz) lard

180ml (6½fl oz) water

1 egg, lightly beaten, for glazing and sealing

Filling

3 rashers of thick bacon

265g (5½oz) pork loin

½ bunch of spring onions, trimmed

1 clove of garlic, peeled

1 tbsp chopped fresh parsley

2 tbsp Calvados or cider

Salt and freshly ground black pepper

8 hard-boiled quail's eggs, peeled (some supermarkets sell cooked peeled ones)

Equipment

12-hole muffin tin

Start by making the pastry. Put the flour, salt, pepper and egg yolk in a large bowl and mix everything together until well combined. Make a well in the middle. Put the butter, lard and water in a small pan over a low heat and let the fat melt. Turn the heat up so that the liquid is bubbling furiously. It is important not to let the water boil before the fat has melted otherwise too much of the water will evaporate, changing the quantities of the liquid.

Remove the pan from the heat and pour this liquid into the well in the middle of the flour mixture. Stir quickly to form a firmish dough. You may not need all of the water. It depends so much on the weather and how thirsty the flour is. Stir it well for a minute or so, then once it has cooled down lift the pastry from the bowl and knead it on a lightly floured work surface so it is smooth and uniform. Wrap the pastry in clingfilm and put in the fridge for a good 30 minutes while you make the filling.

Preheat the oven to 200°C (400°F), Gas Mark 6.

Blitz all the filling ingredients except the quail's eggs in a food processor until minced.

Remove the pastry from the fridge and divide it into two-third and one-third portions. Take the two-thirds piece and divide it into 8 balls. Roll a ball out with your hands, then flatten it into a rough circle bigger than the muffin hole and push it down into the muffin tin. Make sure the pastry goes right into the 'corners' of the tin. Ease up the edges of the pastry so they stand 5mm (¼in) proud of the top of the tin. Repeat with the rest of the pastry balls.

▶

Pork pies with cider *(cont.)*

Put a thin layer of the mince mix in the bottom of the pastry, then take a quail's egg and place it on its side in the middle of the pastry case. Pile more mince mix on top until the pastry is full and has a peak in the middle. Repeat with all the pies.

Take the one-third piece of pastry and divide it into 8 balls. Take one piece and flatten it into a circle large enough to act as a lid for the pies. Brush around the edge of the lid, using the egg wash to act like glue. Place the lid on a pie and squeeze the edges together to seal. Repeat with all the pies. Cut a hole in the top of the pastry for the steam to escape during baking and glaze the top of the pork pies with the beaten egg.

Bake in the oven for 30–35 minutes, or until the pastry is firm and looks golden brown. Serve with some pickle and very cold lager.

Roquefort
Baked Potatoes

Having a snugly duvet-diving day? Can't face the world? This is the comfort food of all comfort foods. The spuds will warm your tummy and calm your mind. The diet can start tomorrow. Serves 4 *(V if veggie cheese is used)*

4 large potatoes

180g (6oz) Roquefort cheese

Freshly ground black pepper

A little milk

1 bunch of fresh chives, finely chopped

Preheat the oven to 220°C (425°F), Gas Mark 7.

Prick the potatoes all over with a fork, then bake in the oven for 1 hour, or until a knife prodded into the thickest part comes out clean. Once baked, remove them from the oven and while the potatoes are still hot, slit them open with a sharp knife. Scoop out all of the insides and place in a pan. Pop the skins back in the oven to keep warm.

Crumble the cheese into the pan, then add some pepper (the cheese is very salty so you will not need any salt) and the milk. Heat through briefly, stirring vigorously with a wooden spoon until smooth. Remove the potato skins from the oven, spoon the filling back in, then sprinkle over the chopped chives.

Excellent with a New World white and a simple green salad.

Sticky glazed
Asian Ham

Perfect summer's day picnic food. Bake a whole joint and, once it's cool, wrap up in foil and put the glaze in a jar. Pack it into the hamper along with crusty bread and other snacky treats, head for the park and pray that the weather will hold! Serves 10 or more

Cured gammon joint or ham joint (I used a 2.5kg (5½lb) ham off the bone)

1 small handful of black peppercorns

2 bay leaves

1cm (½in) piece of fresh ginger, finely grated

1 star anise

1 large handful of cloves

Sticky glaze

2 cloves of garlic, peeled, crushed and squashed

Finely grated zest and juice of ½ orange

220g (7½oz) honey

340g (12oz) soft light brown sugar

1 red chilli, deseeded and finely chopped (optional)

1 tsp Chinese five-spice powder

100ml (4fl oz) soy sauce

Salt and freshly ground black pepper

Cured joints can be very salty, so it's best to soak the joint in cold water overnight. If you're short on time, or just clean forgot to soak it the night before, instead cook the joint in a large pan of water for 40 minutes to get rid of excess salt. Remove from the pan and discard the salted liquid.

Weigh the joint to calculate the cooking time. Place in a clean pan and cover completely with water. Add the peppercorns, bay leaves, ginger, star anise and half the cloves, bring to the boil, then turn down the heat to a simmer. The joint needs 25 minutes simmering time per 450g (1lb) (so mine took 1 hour 50 minutes).

Thirty minutes before the joint is ready, preheat the oven to 220°C (425°F), Gas Mark 7. Mix all the glaze ingredients in a small pan, heat gently to dissolve the sugar, then simmer for 25 minutes until reduced and thickened.

Remove the joint from the water and pat dry with kitchen paper. Keep the cooking liquid, it is delicious. (I boil it like mad to reduce the quantity and increase the flavour, adding carrots, onions, a splash of Madeira and some seasoning for a tummy-warming soup.) Remove the thick layer of skin (but not the fat) from the joint. This can be quite fiddly and often comes off in bits rather than in one large piece. Use a sharp small knife to score the meat diagonally, then change direction and score the other way to form diamonds. Stick the remaining cloves into the holes where the lines cross, then pour the glaze over the meat. Put the joint in the oven and cook for 20–30 minutes, or until the top begins to brown. It can catch easily at this point because of the honey, so keep a close eye on it! Once the joint is cooked, remove from the oven and cover loosely with baking paper to allow it to 'rest'. This evens out the temperature and makes the meat more juicy. Serve with hunks of bread and cold potatoes.

Chicken Pies
with mushroom & tarragon

The bog-standard filling of chicken, peas, carrots and tarragon is a little bit, well 'yawn'. However, throw in a splash of brandy or a smidgeon of white wine (optional, as always) and we can drag this 1970s chicken pie kicking and screaming from the traditions of the pineapple on sticks and devilled eggs to the glory of the 21st-century urban plate. Serves 4

1 quantity of savoury shortcrust (see page 220) or 500g (1lb 2oz) shop-bought shortcrust pastry

1 small chicken, about 1.5kg (3lb 6oz)

1 bay leaf

Few black peppercorns

40g (1½oz) plain flour, plus extra for dusting

1 egg, lightly beaten, for glazing

Few glugs of extra-virgin olive oil

1 large onion, peeled and finely diced

150g (5oz) wild mushrooms, sliced

100ml (4fl oz) brandy (optional)

300ml (11fl oz) chicken stock (this can be taken from the liquid in which the chicken is poached)

200ml (7fl oz) double cream

Small handful of chopped fresh tarragon

Equipment

Four individual dishes, each about 13 x 17cm (5¼ x 6¾in). Capacity about 300ml (11fl oz)

If using homemade pastry, follow the recipe on page 220.

Put the chicken in a large pot and cover it with cold water. Add the bay leaf and peppercorns and bring to just under the boil. Once it reaches this stage turn the temperature down so the water is just poaching – a bubble should just break the surface now and then. Poach for about 1 hour, or until the chicken is cooked through. If any frothy scum floats to the surface then just spoon it off.

Roll the pastry out on a lightly floured work surface to just larger than the pie dish then place in the fridge for about 30 minutes, or until firm. To make the top look even more appealing, cut out some pastry leaves from the trimmings to put on top. Place these in the fridge. Brush the top of each dish with a little beaten egg and stick a rim of pastry from the trimmings, about 1cm (½in) wide, along the top. This will help the pastry lid to stick on and not slide off during cooking.

Remove the chicken from the poaching liquor. Sieve out the peppercorns and bay leaf from the liquid and set aside.

Heat some oil in a lidded sauté pan over a gentle heat, add the onion and a little water and cook until the onion turns translucent and soft, but with no colour. Add the mushrooms and cook for a couple more minutes. Turn up the heat, add the brandy, if using, and boil for 2 minutes.

Meanwhile, put the flour in a small pan and gradually add 50ml (2fl oz) of the chicken stock, stirring all the time so the mixture does not go lumpy. Add this to the onions, mushrooms and brandy mixture, then add 250ml

▶

Chicken pies with mushroom & tarragon *(cont.)*

(9fl oz) of the chicken stock poaching liquid together with the cream. Boil until the mixture has reduced by half.

While the mixture is reducing, take the now-cooled chicken and remove all the flesh in large bite-sized chunks and set aside.

Once the onion mixture has reduced by half, season the chicken with salt and pepper then add it and the tarragon to the onion mixture. Cook through for 5 minutes then remove the pan from the heat and pour it into the pie dish. Brush some beaten egg along the pastry rim.

Place the rolled out pastry on top of the chicken, pressing it down well at the edges to stick to the egg. Flute the edges with your fingers or use a fork to make a pattern around the edge of the pie. Brush the pastry liberally with the beaten egg to give it a shiny glaze when it comes out of the oven.

Bake the pie for about 25 minutes, or until the pastry is golden brown and firm.

Serve with minted green peas doused in butter, salt and pepper.

Save the rest of the chicken stock if there is any left. Put it on the heat in a wide-based pan and boil it until it reduces by half. Remove the pan from the heat and leave to cool, then pour it into an ice-cube tray and pop it into the freezer. Chicken stock, just when you need it.

Baked Plaice

with rosemary & anchovies

I grow my own rosemary for this dish at home. It has a tendency to grow like wildfire. While all other plants seem to wither and die the moment they cross the threshold of my house, dear old rosemary just keeps on growing. Serves 4

4 large plaice fillets, skinned

Salt and freshly ground black pepper

4 anchovy fillets, drained and roughly chopped

4 long sprigs of fresh rosemary, each about 10cm (4in), leaves removed from lower stem

2 tbsp extra-virgin olive oil

150ml (5fl oz) white wine

6 cloves of garlic, peeled and bruised

Finely grated zest of 1 lime, plus 1 lime, cut into quarters

Big knob of butter (optional)

Preheat the oven to 170°C (325°F), Gas Mark 3.

Season the plaice with a little salt and pepper (because you are using anchovies, which are already very salty, not much extra salt will be needed). Sprinkle the anchovies on top, then roll the plaice up from top to tail and secure each fillet by piercing with a long sprig of rosemary. Place them in a small roasting tin. Sprinkle the oil over the fillets, pour on the white wine and scatter the garlic cloves around. Sprinkle the lime zest over the top and cook in the oven for 15–20 minutes, or until the fish looks just translucent and flakes easily.

Once cooked, put a small knob of butter on each fillet for extra flavour, if you wish, along with a lime quarter for stunning presentation. Serve with baby vegetables.

Pumpkin & chestnut
Empanadas

These are made with beautiful thyme and polenta pastry, which has a crisp, crunchy texture and just melts on your tongue. If you are pressed for time, a pack of shop-bought shortcrust will suffice, but when rolling it out, sprinkle a handful of polenta and fresh thyme onto it between each roll for a similar effect. Makes about 6 (V)

Thyme and polenta pastry (see page 221) or 500g (1lb 2oz) shop-bought shortcrust pastry

1–2 tbsp extra-virgin olive oil

1 medium onion, peeled and diced

Large wedge of pumpkin or 1 small squash, peeled, deseeded and diced

140g (5oz) sweet chestnuts (in frozen veggie section or special ingredients section of the supermarket)

1 clove of garlic, peeled and finely chopped

Small handful of chopped fresh thyme leaves

Handful of pine nuts, toasted (see page 44)

Small handful of raisins

Salt and freshly ground black pepper

Plain flour or cornmeal, for dusting

1 egg, lightly beaten

Equipment

Large round cutter, about 11cm (4½in) in diameter

First, make the pastry following the recipe on page 221. Wrap the dough in clingfilm and put in the fridge for about 30 minutes, or until firm.

Preheat the oven to 200°C (400°F), Gas Mark 6.

For the filling, heat the oil in a sauté pan or large frying pan over a medium heat, add the onion and cook for about 8 minutes, or until it begins to soften. Add the pumpkin and cook until it is soft. Add the chestnuts, garlic and thyme and cook for another minute. Add the pine nuts and raisins and stir well. Season to taste with salt and pepper then remove the pan from the heat and leave to cool.

Remove the pastry from the fridge and roll it out to a thickness of half a £1 coin. If using the thyme and polenta pastry roll the dough out on a lightly floured work surface, but if using shop-bought shortcrust then roll it out on a handful of cornmeal so that the cornmeal sticks to the pastry.

Using the large round cutter, cut out 6 rounds. If you don't have a cutter of this size use a saucer or the bottom of a cake tin as a template, place it on the pastry and then cut round it with a knife. Put the pastry rounds on a large flat baking tray. If there is any pastry leftover, scrunch it up and re-roll it to make another round. There is ample filling in this recipe for an extra one.

Brush a 1cm (½in) border of lightly beaten egg all around the pastry border. Dollop a good spoonful of the filling mixture on one half of the pastry rounds and fold the empty half of the pastry over the filling. Press

▶

Pumpkin & chestnut empanadas (cont.)

down along the edges firmly and then use your thumb and forefinger of one hand and the forefinger of the other to pinch round the edges, creating a 'fluted' edge. This is the way I like to do it but as long as the edges are sealed it doesn't matter how it is done. Repeat with all the pastry rounds, then put the baking tray in the fridge for 20 minutes to firm up if the pastry is too soft.

Once the pastry is firm, remove it from the fridge and brush some more beaten egg all over them. Bake in the oven for 20 minutes, or until the pastry is firm and golden brown.

Serve hot or cold with lemon wedges and a salad. This is another great one for your vegetarian friends.

Quick Chicken
with lemon, thyme & butternut squash

When you can't face the rigours of making a full Sunday roast, this shortcut baked chicken will not disappoint. Serves 4

2–3 tbsp extra-virgin olive oil

8 chicken pieces (I like a mixture of thighs and whole legs, skin on)

Salt and freshly ground black pepper

1 butternut squash, peeled, deseeded and cut into large chunks

2 sprigs of chopped fresh rosemary

1 handful of fresh thyme leaves

8 cloves of garlic, unpeeled but squashed

Finely grated zest of 1 lemon

1 glass of white wine

2 tbsp plain flour

300ml (11fl oz) chicken stock (you can buy fresh chicken stock from supermarkets)

Preheat the oven to 220°C (425°F), Gas Mark 7. Drizzle oil over the chicken pieces and season them with salt and pepper. Put them skin-side down in a roasting tin and cook for 10 minutes.

In another roasting tin, put the squash, drizzle with the oil and set aside.

Remove the chicken from the oven. Turn the oven down to 170°C (325°F), Gas Mark 3 and turn the chicken pieces skin-side up. Sprinkle both the squash and the chicken with the rosemary, thyme, garlic and lemon zest, then put them both in the oven and cook for 30 minutes, or until the chicken is cooked through. To check this, make a tiny cut in the thickest part of the chicken. If the juices run clear then the meat is ready, any pinkness and cook the chicken for a further 10 minutes.

Remove the chicken from the oven and place the pieces on a plate together with the garlic cloves. Cover the plate with baking paper and set aside to 'rest'.

Meanwhile, make the sauce. Tip away all but 2 tablespoons of the fat from the chicken juices in the tin. Place the roasting tin on the hob over a medium heat, add the wine and cook until the mixture had reduced to 3 tablespoons. Stir in the flour well, making sure there are no lumps. Next, add the stock stirring all the time. Bring the mixture to the boil, then remove from the heat. Pass the mixture through the sieve, taste the liquid, season if necessary then serve with the chicken. Remove the squash from the oven, drizzle with a little more oil to prevent it drying out, and serve immediately with the chicken.

Serve with some homegrown curly kale (it grows like a mad plant and requires very little attention) or emerald-green crunchy spinach.

Pastilla
(chicken pie, Moroccan style)

One of the best things about Morocco is its awesome food. It is spicy, smoky, aromatic and sweet, and there is always lots of it. For this recipe I buy chicken thighs with the bone in and then skin and bone them myself at home. Much cheaper and good to get stuck in with your butchery skills. Serves 4

2 tbsp veg oil and 2 tbsp water, plus extra for oiling

8–10 chicken thighs, bone in

2 large onions, peeled and finely chopped

2 cloves of garlic, peeled and finely chopped

4cm (1½in) piece of fresh ginger

1 heaped tbsp ground ginger

1 heaped tbsp ground cinnamon

1 heaped tbsp ground coriander

Pinch of saffron threads

2 big squidges of honey

Finely grated zest of 1 lemon

2 handfuls of flaked almonds, toasted (see page 44)

1 bunch of fresh coriander, roughly chopped

Salt and freshly ground black pepper

270g (10oz) shop-bought filo pastry

115g (4oz) butter, melted

3 eggs, beaten

Icing sugar, for dredging

Oil the cake tin. Remove the bones from the chicken pieces and slice the meat into chunks.

Heat the oil in a frying pan over a gentle heat, add the onions and fry for about 10–15 minutes, or until they turn translucent, softened, but with no colour. Add the garlic and fry for a further 1 minute. Remove the onions with a slotted spoon and set aside.

Add a little more oil to the pan, add the chicken and fry quickly to brown it. Do this in 2–3 batches so the pan does not get overcrowded and just 'steam' the meat.

Once the chicken is cooked, return it to the pan, grate in the ginger and add the ground ginger, cinnamon, ground coriander, saffron, honey and lemon zest. Cook for 1 minute then stir in the flaked almonds and chopped coriander. Season to taste with salt and pepper. Remove the pan from the heat and set aside.

Brush each piece of filo liberally with melted butter to prevent it from burning in the oven and then layer the pastry over the base of the pan

▶

23cm (9in) springform cake tin or deep sandwich tin

and up the sides so that pieces of filo overlap, drape over and hang down the edges of the pan. For extra safety do about 5 layers.

Tip the chicken mixture into the pastry and spread it out evenly, then pour the beaten eggs on to the chicken. Fold the draped-over pieces of filo on top of the pie. Brush some more filo pastry sheets with butter, then scrunch them up and place them on top of the pastilla.

Dredge the pie with icing sugar and bake in the oven for 20 minutes, or until the pastry is golden brown and crisp.

Leave to cool for 1 minute before gently removing the pie from the tin to a serving plate with a large spatula.

Serve on a rug, with boiled buttered carrots tossed in cumin and butter and a glass of hot sugary mint tea.

Fish Pie

You just can't beat a good fish pie. Perfectly poached, creamy fish with a thick, velvety mash topping. This dish is one of the more involved ones and so you'll need to set aside a bit of time to make it. Serves 4–6

4 large floury potatoes, such as Maris Piper, Desiree or King Edward

2 tbsp crème fraîche

60g (2½oz) butter

Salt and freshly ground black pepper

500ml (18fl oz) milk

1 bay leaf

6 black peppercorns

2 sprigs of fresh thyme

2 stalks of fresh parsley

1 large onion, peeled, halved and finely sliced

340g (12oz) haddock fillet, skinned and de-boned

400g (14oz) salmon fillet, skinned

125g (4½oz) peeled ready-cooked prawns

2 eggs

200ml (7fl oz) double cream

40g (1½oz) plain flour

1 bunch of fresh parsley, leaves only, roughly chopped

80g (3oz) breadcrumbs

Equipment

Large casserole dish

Preheat the oven to 220°C (425°F), Gas Mark 7.

Prick the potatoes a couple of times with a fork and bake for 1 hour, or until a knife goes through the flesh easily with little resistance. Remove from the oven, squeeze the flesh out into a bowl and mix with the crème fraîche and 20g (¾oz) of the butter. Season to taste with salt and pepper and set aside.

While the potatoes are cooking, pour the milk into a sauté pan, add the bay leaf, peppercorns, thyme, parsley stalks and onion and add the fish, skin-side down. Bring gently up to a low boil then immediately turn down to a simmer. Cook for 7–8 minutes, or until the fish is cooked through. The flesh will look opaque and shiny.

Remove the fish from the sauté pan with a slotted spoon and flake the fish gently with your hands into large chunks into the base of the casserole dish. Add the cooked prawns.

Strain the liquid through a sieve into a bowl. Discard the herbs, onion and peppercorns. Measure the cooking liquid plus enough cream to make it up to 600ml (1 pint).

▶

Put the eggs in a small pan of boiling water and cook for 7 minutes. Drain immediately, rinse with cool water, peel and set aside. Wipe out the small pan and put back on a medium heat ready to make the fish pie sauce. Put the 40g (1½oz) flour and remaining 40g (1½oz) butter into the pan and cook, stirring, for 1 minute. Remove the pan from the heat and gradually add the milk and cream cooking liquid, bit by bit, stirring all the time to avoid lumps.

Return the pan to the heat, stirring all the time and bring to the boil. Boil for a couple of minutes. The sauce will have thickened. Taste the sauce and season with salt and pepper, then roughly chop the eggs and add them to the sauce, mixing well. Pour the sauce all over the fish and sprinkle over the chopped parsley. Pile the potato mix on top of the fish. I take large spoonfuls and dollop them in a rough pattern then fluff them up with a fork. Sprinkle the potatoes with breadcrumbs and cook in the oven for 20–25 minutes, or until the top is golden brown and crunchy.

I know some cooks who put peas and what not in a fish pie. However, I like to serve it with a pile of peas on the side with a knob of butter slipping down the veg. This is a real family meal and so good served with the dish in the middle of the table for everyone to dig in and help themselves.

Incredibly naughty mini
Toad-in-the-Hole

Crunchy, tender toad-in-the-hole, made in individual portions and flavoured with mustard, sage and cider. Batter never tasted so good. Serves 4

Vegetable oil, for oiling

2 eggs

115g (4oz) plain flour

Mustard powder, to taste

3 sage leaves, or thyme if you prefer, finely chopped

150ml (5fl oz) soured cream

150ml (5fl oz) milk

18 Cumberland sausages, each cut in half

1 tbsp cider (optional)

Salt and freshly ground black pepper

Equipment

12-hole muffin tin

Ovenproof baking dish

Preheat oven to 200°C (400°F), Gas Mark 6. Oil the muffin tin.

Whisk the eggs in a large bowl until frothy. In a separate bowl, put the flour, mustard and sage, then make a hole in the middle. Gradually add the soured cream and milk. Mix together lightly. Add the eggs and stir a little to combine, then leave the batter to stand for 30 minutes or so.

Put the sausages in an ovenproof dish and cook in the oven for 25–30 minutes, or according to the packet instructions, then set aside.

Add the cider, if using, to the batter, stir for 10 seconds, then pour the mixture into a measuring jug (makes it so much easier to pour into the muffin tin). Divide the mixture among the muffin holes (it makes around 12) then put 3 sausage halves into each hole, sticking up with the uncut side down. Cook in the oven for 20–25 minutes, or until puffed up and golden brown. As soon as they are cooked, remove from the oven, leave for 1 minute then bang the tin on the surface to loosen them from the holes.

Serve with gravy.

Prosciutto, mozzarella & fig
Pizza

A quintessential flavour combination on a simple-to-make pizza base. It is good to make several of these bases in one go and then freeze them, so that next time pizza is on the menu, a base can be quickly defrosted and finished with toppings. Serves 4

250g (9oz) strong white bread flour, plus extra for dusting

1 tsp salt

½ tsp fast-action dried yeast

125–145ml (4½–5fl oz) warm water

30ml (1¼fl oz) extra-virgin olive oil, plus extra for oiling and drizzling

Pizza topping

1 tube of good tomato purée

250g (9oz) mozzarella cheese

8 slices of prosciutto, ripped up into bite-sized pieces

5 figs, quartered

Salt and freshly ground black pepper

1 bunch of fresh basil

Equipment

Very large baking tray, or a 30cm (12in) pizza plate

Mix the flour, salt and yeast together in a large bowl and make a well in the middle. In a jug, mix the water and oil together, then pour this into the well of the flour mixture and mix to make a soft but not sticky dough. Knead for 10 minutes by hand on a lightly floured work surface or for 5 minutes in an electric mixer fitted with a dough hook. Bring the dough together to a smooth flat ball and place on a large, lightly floured baking tray. Roll it out as flat as you can.

Cover the pizza dough loosely with oiled clingfilm, making sure it is airtight. Leave in a warm but not hot place for 30–40 minutes.

Preheat the oven to 220°C (425°F), Gas Mark 7.

Remove the clingfilm from the dough and roll out to a 30cm (12in) circle to knock some air out, then prick holes all over the dough with a fork. Spread over the tomato purée, leaving a 2.5cm (1in) border, followed by the mozzarella, prosciutto and half the figs. Drizzle with oil and season with salt and pepper. Bake in the oven for 15–20 minutes, or until the bread is crisp and golden brown and the cheese has melted. Scatter basil over the top and arrange the remaining figs on the pizza. Drizzle with oil.

Serve at the centre of the table so everyone can rip off their piece of Italian gold.

Steak Pies

with wild mushrooms & Madeira

These pies have a great-tasting sauce and well-risen puff pastry with no sogginess. Any dried mushrooms will do, but the best are morels for their intensely smoky, woody flavour. They can be fairly pricey, so when my pockets aren't feeling so deep, I use porcini mushrooms instead. Serves 4

1 quantity of puff pastry (see page 218) or 500g (1lb 2oz) shop-bought puff pastry

Plain flour

600ml (21fl oz) good beef stock

200ml (7fl oz) Madeira

Few glugs of extra-virgin olive oil

1 large onion, peeled and cut into chunks

1 clove of garlic, peeled and crushed

2 sprigs of fresh rosemary, leaves only, finely chopped

1 small bunch of fresh thyme, leaves only

Salt and freshly ground black pepper

1kg (2¼lb) chuck steak, excess fat and sinew removed, cut into chunks

50g (2oz) butter

25g (1oz) dried mushrooms

1 egg, lightly beaten

Equipment

Four individual dishes, each about 13 x 17cm (5¼ x 6¾in) about 300ml (11fl oz) capacity

Preheat the oven to 190°C (375°F), Gas Mark 5.

If making homemade pastry, make it according to the recipe on page 218. Roll the puff pastry out on a floured work surface to about 5mm (¼in) thick. Cut out 4 lids for your pie dishes just a little bigger than the top of the pie dishes and arrange on a baking tray. Cut out some leaves for decoration from the excess pastry and place on top of the pastry pie lids then put them into the fridge for about 30 minutes, or until firm.

Mix the stock and Madeira together in a jug.

Heat a glug of olive oil in a sauté pan over a gentle heat, add the onion and fry for about 10 minutes, or until it begins to go translucent. Add the garlic, rosemary and thyme and cook for a further 1 minute. Remove the onion mixture with a slotted spoon and put into a bowl. Heat a little more oil in the pan.

Meanwhile, put some flour in a bowl and season well with salt and pepper. Toss the meat in the flour, then put one-third of the meat in the sauté pan and cook until browned on all sides. Tip into the bowl with the onions and continue to brown the rest of the meat, adding the meat to the bowl when it is browned. Reserve any leftover seasoned flour.

Place the empty pan back on the heat. Pour in a mugful of the stock mixture and boil for 30 seconds, scraping off any sediment from the base of the pan with a wooden spoon. Pour this mixture into the bowl containing the meat and set aside. (If you have black bits on the bottom of the pan leftover from the meat, skip this step and clean out the pan first, otherwise the pie will taste burnt.)

▶

Add the butter to the pan and a couple of tablespoons of the seasoned flour. Gradually add the reserved stock mixture stirring all the time. If the sauce looks lumpy at any time, whisk and beat the mixture like mad. The lumps will eventually disappear – it does take a bit of elbow grease though. Bring the mixture to the boil for 1 minute, then turn down the heat and add the meat and onion mixture together with the mushrooms. Taste the stew, seasoning with salt and pepper if necessary. Divide among the pie dishes and cook in the oven for 1 hour.

After an hour, turn the oven up to 200°C (400°F), Gas Mark 6. If the meat is looking a bit dry, add some hot water to keep it moist. Take the puff pastry from the fridge and brush it with the beaten egg. Just brush the top liberally but not the sides as the egg may stick the puff pastry layers together and it will not rise as well.

Cook the pastry for 20–30 minutes, or until the pastry is well risen, golden brown and the sides are firm. Remove the pie dishes and pastry from the oven and place a piece of pastry on top of the dish as a lid.

Best served on a winter day in your favourite local with boiled potatoes and minted peas.

Desserts & Patisserie

When I sit down for a big meal, my mind is focused largely on dessert. Few people can resist a piping hot crumble with a rich, buttery topping and soft, sweet fruit below; or a doughy jam roly poly with a steaming hot puddle of custard. Enjoy my stunning pear tarte tartin – its beauty and exquisite taste steal my heart every time I make it, or try The Skinny Tarts, which are quick to prepare, easy on the palate and extremely kind to one's waistline.

'*Life is uncertain. Eat dessert first.*'

Ernestine Ulmer
Writer
1925 –

Dark chocolate & raspberry swirl
Cheesecake

This dessert requires a couple of hours' setting time, but if, like me, you aren't blessed with oodles of patience, put the glasses in the freezer for half an hour to speed things up.
Serves 4 *(V)*

140g (5oz) digestive biscuits, crushed

100g (3½oz) butter, melted

1 tbsp brown sugar

100ml (3½oz) double cream

25g (1oz) icing sugar

200g (7oz) cream cheese

100g (3½oz) good (at least 64% cocoa solids or more) dark chocolate, melted

200g (7oz or 1 punnet) raspberries

40g (1½oz) white chocolate, shaved with a vegetable peeler, to decorate

Equipment

4 very large wine glasses or tumblers

Mix the biscuits, butter and brown sugar together in a large bowl and divide among the glasses.

Whip the double cream and icing sugar together in a large bowl until it is very thick and can hold its shape in the bowl. Put the cream cheese in another bowl and stir well to loosen it up a bit, then put a dollop of the double cream into the cream cheese, mix and stir well. Add the rest of the double cream and mix until it is all combined.

Spoon a dollop of the mixture equally among the wine glasses, then add a dollop of the melted dark chocolate over the top and leave to cool slightly until thick. Add another dollop of the cream cheese mixture and stir the chocolate into the cream using only two 'turns' of the spoon so the dark of the chocolate and the white of the cream looks marbled and the bottom layer of the cream cheese is left white.

Top with the raspberries and white chocolate shavings, to decorate.

Bakewell Tart

Are you a pudding or are you a tart? The foodie cognoscenti are still debating this question when it comes to La Bakewell and no one is able to agree. This particular tart (for that's what I choose to call it) is finished with toasted flaked almonds, but for a more old-school, just-dropped-round-to-granny's-house feel, top with some bright white fondant icing and plonk a spanking red cherry right in the middle. Glorious. Serves 8 (V)

500g (1lb 2oz) shop-bought shortcrust pastry or Lemon and almond pastry (see page 222)

Frangipane

200g (7oz) butter

200g (7oz) caster sugar

2 eggs

2 tbsp amaretto

40g (1½oz) plain flour

200g (7oz) ground almonds

40g (1½oz) flaked almonds

Filling

180g (6½oz) good strawberry jam, preferably homemade

Equipment

23cm (9in) flan ring or loose-bottomed tart tin, about 4cm (1½in) deep

Roll out the pastry on a lightly floured work surface to just under the thickness of a £1 coin. If using a flan ring, put it on a baking tray. Lower the pastry into the ring or tin and ease down into the sides and corners. Place in the fridge for about 30 minutes, or until firm.

Preheat the oven to 180°C (350°F), Gas Mark 4.

Once the pastry is firm, remove it from the fridge, take a piece of baking paper slightly larger than the tart and scrunch it up, then unscrunch it and line the tart with it, taking it right up the sides. Fill it with baking beans or dried beans and 'blind bake' in the oven for 15–20 minutes, until the edges are light brown and the base is dry to the touch. Remove the baking beans and paper and cook for a further 3–4 minutes, until golden. Remove from the oven and set aside.

Meanwhile, make the frangipane. Put the butter and sugar in a large bowl and cream together until pale and fluffy. Gradually add the eggs and the Amaretto. Fold in the flour and the ground almonds.

Spread the jam over the base of the pastry case, then spoon in the frangipane and smooth with a palette knife. Sprinkle the flaked almonds on top and bake in the oven for 30–35 minutes, or until the frangipane has puffed up slightly. Check after 15 minutes, if the edges of the pastry are browning too much, cover with foil to prevent further colouring.

Remove the tart from the oven and leave to cool. The top may look as if it has cracked slightly, but this is the way it should look. Cut into small slices as part of an afternoon tea, or simply serve with single cream.

Banoffee Pie

I had thought this creamy pie was from the US, but no … it's one of ours. A cream pie/cheesecake hybrid with lashings of sticky toffee and rum-laced bananas, it also has the advantage of being an utter doddle to make. Serves 6–8 *(V)*

Toffee layer

1 x 400g (14oz) can of condensed milk (or a can of pre-made caramel)

Biscuit base

180g (6½oz) digestive biscuits, crushed

100g (3½oz) butter, melted

Banana layer

25g (1oz) butter

3 bananas, sliced

3 tbsp rum (optional)

Seeds of ½ vanilla pod or 2 drops of vanilla extract

Cream topping

300ml (11fl oz) whipping cream

1 tbsp icing sugar

Seeds of ½ vanilla pod or 2 drops of vanilla extract

Equipment

23cm (9in) deep flan ring or loose-bottomed cake tin

To make the toffee layer, put the can of condensed milk in a medium pan, cover it with water and boil for 2 hours. Tedious I know, but worth it in the tasty stakes. If you have a can of pre-made caramel you can skip this step.

Meanwhile, for the base, put the biscuits and melted butter into a large bowl and mix together, then press into the flan ring or tin. Put in the fridge for about 30 minutes, or until firm.

To make the banana layer, melt the butter in a medium pan, add the bananas, rum and vanilla and cook for a few minutes until the bananas have softened slightly. Set aside.

For the cream, whip the whipping cream, vanilla and icing sugar until it begins to thicken then set aside. Put the mixture in the fridge for about 30 minutes, or until set.

To assemble, remove the biscuit base from the fridge. Spoon the caramel or condensed milk over the base and then layer over the bananas. Tip the whipped cream over the pie and spread it over to cover completely. Put the pie in the fridge for 30 minutes before serving.

Serve with a hot chocolate sauce (see page 172).

Chocolate
Melting Puds

These little naughties are always crowd pleasers. They're good for dinner parties, as they can be prepared ahead of time and left in the fridge until ready to bake. The trick is to get the outside cooked but the inside still hot and gooey. Serves 4 (V)

110g (4oz) butter, plus 40g (1½oz) butter, melted for greasing

1 tbsp cocoa powder

110g (4oz) caster sugar, plus 1 tbsp for coating

110g (4oz) good (at least 64% cocoa solids or more) dark chocolate, finely chopped or grated

2 eggs

2 egg yolks

110g (4oz) plain flour

Equipment

4 dariole moulds, about 8cm (3in) at the widest point and just under 5.5cm (2½in) high

Grease the dariole moulds with the 40g (1½oz) of melted butter. Mix the cocoa powder and tablespoon of caster sugar in a bowl, then put the mixture in the moulds, tilting and turning them so the mixture sticks to the butter. Tip out any excess.

Melt the rest of the butter in a small pan over a medium heat. Remove the pan from the heat, add the chocolate and leave it to melt.

Preheat the oven to 180°C (350°F), Gas Mark 4. Whisk the eggs and yolks in a large bowl until they start to thicken, then gradually add the sugar in 2–3 additions, whisking all the time. The mixture should become thick, pale and mousse-like. Stir the melted chocolate and butter mixture then gradually pour it into the whisked eggs, whisking all the time. The chocolate is heavy and sinks to the bottom so check none is hiding! Sift in the flour and whisk briefly to combine.

Divide the mixture among the prepared moulds and bake for 10–12 minutes. The tops should be firm and the middle should remain molten.

Once the puds are ready, leave to cool for a minute or two, then use oven gloves to place a serving plate upside down on top of the mould. Hold everything tightly together and turn the whole lot over so the plate is now on the bottom. Put the plate on the work surface and gently shake the mould until the pudding plops out. If you find it refuses to come out (these puds can be notoriously stubborn) take a small knife and run it between the mould and the pudding to loosen it a little.

Even if your middle is not molten, the dessert is still totally delicious. Serve with sweetened crème fraîche.

Pear Tarte Tatin

The doyenne of all tarts. To make your tarte palate-perfect, take the time to really caramelise the pears prior to baking in the oven. Serves 8–10 *(V)*

1 quantity of puff pastry (see page 218) or 500g (1lb 2oz) shop-bought puff pastry

100g (3½oz) butter

100g (3½oz) caster sugar

5–6 large equal-sized pears, peeled, cored and halved

Plain flour, for dusting

Finely grated zest of ½ lemon

Equipment

Ovenproof frying pan or 20cm (8in) loose-bottomed cake tin

Preheat the oven to 200°C (400°F), Gas Mark 6.

If using homemade pastry, follow the recipe on page 218.

Melt the butter and sugar in an ovenproof frying pan over a low heat. Once the butter has melted and the sugar has dissolved, turn up the heat and let it boil. The mixture will begin to look like it has curdled and look very oily, but just swirl the pan around and keep heating it until the mixture goes a honeycomb colour. This process takes about 8–10 minutes. Remove the pan from the heat and carefully lower the pears into the mixture. The hot sugar mixture can splash up and burn badly so do this carefully. Return the pan to the heat and cook over a high heat for 5–6 minutes, spooning the caramel mixture over the pears every now and then so the pears are fully caramelised and going golden brown. The more colour, the more flavour. It may seem that the sugar is about to burn, but the juice from the pears will prevent this from happening.

Remove the pan from the heat, and using a knife and fork (just to ease the fruit around rather than stab it!), arrange the fruit cut-side up with the pointed end in the middle. The pears will look like the spokes of a wheel. Set aside. If your frying pan is not ovenproof then arrange the pears in the cake tin instead.

Roll the pastry out on a lightly floured work surface to the thickness of a £1 coin and cut out a circle large enough to sit snugly in the frying pan or tin. Sprinkle the lemon zest over the top, then place the pastry over

▶

Pear tarte Tatin *(cont.)*

the fruit. Tuck the edges down the side of the fruit, so the pears are enclosed, and bake in the oven for 25–30 minutes, or until the pastry has risen nicely.

Remove from the oven and leave the tarte to cool for 5 minutes, then tip off any excess liquid. You can discard this or save it to have with some other fruit – it is so scrummy.

At this point cookbooks always say 'invert the tarte onto a serving plate' and they make it sound so effortless. I do it like this: using oven gloves and standing over the sink (it usually leaks, even with the excess liquid drained off), I take a serving plate that is larger than the frying pan and place it upside down on top of the pan. Then, holding both the pan and the plate tight together, flip everything upside down so the plate is the right way up and the pan is on top. Then, hey presto, lift off the pan and the tarte remains on the plate.

The only thing to serve this with is a rich, vanillary ice cream.

Jam Roly Poly

I love a good Jam Roly Poly – doughy pastry with lashings of just-a-bit-too-hot jam. Memories of primary school stick firmly in my mind, and the current of excitement that would sweep through the classroom on the realisation that Jam Roly Poly would be making an appearance at lunch. This recipe uses beef suet but veggie suet works well too. Serves 6

260g (9oz) self-raising flour, plus extra for dusting

130g (4½oz) ready grated suet

Pinch of salt

2 tbsp caster sugar, plus extra for sprinkling

Finely grated zest of ½ lemon

1 egg

About 4–6 tbsp water

Filling

100g (3½oz) good-quality strawberry or raspberry jam (if thick, heat it first to make more spreadable)

1 tbsp Kirsch (optional)

Fill a roasting tin with water and place on the oven floor. This will create a steamy atmosphere in which to cook the jam roly poly. Preheat the oven to 180°C (360°F), Gas Mark 4.

In a bowl, mix the jam and the Kirsch, if using, and set aside.

Put the flour, suet, salt, caster sugar and lemon zest in a bowl. Stir in the egg and enough water to make a soft, smooth, pliable dough that is not too sticky. Remove the dough from the bowl and knead on a lightly floured work surface for a couple of minutes to make it uniform, then roll out to a rectangle about 20 x 40cm (8 x 16in). You can put the pastry on a piece of baking paper to help roll it up, if you like. Spread the rectangle with jam, leaving a 2cm (¾in) border around all edges.

With the shortest edge facing you, brush the opposite edge with a little water. Roll the pastry up and press the join firmly to seal. Pinch the ends to seal in the jam. Put the roll in a baking tin lined with baking paper, making sure the sealed edge is underneath. Sprinkle with caster sugar, then cover loosely with foil and bake in the oven for 25 minutes. Remove the foil and cook for a further 10–15 minutes, or until the pastry is firm and smells cooked.

Serve with shop-bought custard (the cheap yellow kind), for there is no other way. Jam roly poly doesn't do crème anglaise!

Chocolate
Hazelnut Tart

Double trouble chocolate. A rich chocolate tart filled with gooey squidgy choco-hazelnut mousse filling. The chocolate pastry is good enough to eat on its own like a cookie. The filling can be put in ramekins and cooked for 8 minutes as a quickie dessert, too. This tart is obscenely rich, so each person needs only a sliver to satisfy. Serves 16 (serve small slices as this tart is très, très rich) *(V)*

Chocolate pastry

2 egg yolks

Seeds of 1 vanilla pod or 2 drops of vanilla extract

100g (3½oz) caster sugar

100g (3½oz) butter, softened

165g (5½oz) plain flour, plus extra for dusting

40g (1½oz) good cocoa powder

Pinch of salt

Chocolate filling

100g (3½oz) butter

100g (3½oz) good (at least 60% cocoa solids or more) dark chocolate, grated

1 egg

2 egg yolks

130g (4½oz) caster sugar

60g (2½oz) plain flour

80g (3oz) hazelnuts, chopped and toasted (see page 44), plus a handful for sprinkling

▼

To make the pastry, put the egg yolks, vanilla and sugar in a bowl and mix together. Add the butter and mix briefly until well combined. Add the flour, cocoa powder and the salt and, using your hands, mix together to make a soft dough. Use as few strokes as possible to bring the mixture together and uniform. This way the pastry will remain crumbly and tender when cooked.

Scoop up the pastry with your hand and bring together to form a ball. Wrap the pastry in clingfilm and put in the fridge for 30 minutes.

Preheat the oven to 200°C (400°F), Gas Mark 6.

Remove the pastry from the fridge and roll it out on a lightly floured work surface to a thickness of half a £1 coin. Line the tart tin with the pastry. Take a small ball of pastry rolled in flour (about the size of a 1p) and use it to ease the pastry into the 'corners' of the tart tin. Using a sharp knife, cut off the excess pastry around the top of the tin then run a small sharp knife around the edge between the pastry and the tin to loosen slightly. This will make it much easier to unmould it once it is cooked. Any remaining pastry can be used to make small biscuits or the dough can be wrapped up and frozen for up to a month. Place the tart tin in the fridge for 10 minutes.

Once the pastry is firm, remove it from the fridge. Take a piece of baking paper slightly larger than the tart tin and scrunch it up, then unscrunch it and place it in the tin. Fill the baking paper with baking beans or dried beans and 'blind bake' in the oven for 20 minutes, or until the pastry feels firm to the touch.

▶

Equipment

23cm (9in) loose-bottomed tart tin, about 3cm (1¼in) high

Once cooked, remove from the oven and turn the oven down to 160°C (315°F), Gas Mark 2–3. Remove the baking beans and baking paper and leave to cool.

For the filling, melt the butter in a small pan over a low heat. Remove from the heat, add the grated chocolate and stir well to combine. While this is melting whisk the egg and yolks until they go really pale and frothy, then gradually add the sugar, whisking all the time until the mixture becomes even lighter and more fluffy. Pour the chocolate mixture into the egg mixture, around the sides rather than the middle so the air, which has been whisked in, does not get knocked out. Fold everything together slowly and gently, keeping in as much air as possible. Fold in the flour and then gently fold in the toasted hazelnuts.

Spoon the mixture into the tart case and bake in the oven for 18–20 minutes. The top will be just set and the inside still gooey. If the edges of your pastry are going too dark, put foil over them to prevent further colouring.

Leave the tart to cool for 5 minutes. Use oven gloves to push the base to remove it from the tin, then run a palette knife underneath the tart to loosen if necessary. Leaving it in the tin to cool completely makes it very difficult to remove in one piece. If it does get stuck, it is perfectly acceptable to serve the tart in the tin. Sprinkle with the handful of hazelnuts before serving with slightly whipped cream sweetened with a couple of tablespoons of icing sugar.

Peach Clafoutis

Plums, cherries, nectarines; many different fruits can be used to make this dish. While it's not the prettiest dessert in the pack, the combination of peach and amaretto is a taste not to be missed. Serves 6–8 *(V)*

Vegetable oil or oil spray, for oiling

3–4 just-ripe medium peaches, halved and stoned

4 eggs, plus 3 egg yolks

Seeds of 1 vanilla pod or 2 tsp vanilla extract

100g (3½oz) caster sugar

40g (1½oz) plain flour

Pinch of salt

150ml (5fl oz) double cream

140g (5oz) soured cream or full-fat crème fraîche

2 tbsp amaretto

Icing sugar, for dusting

Equipment

A shallow round or oval pie dish, about 23cm (9in) wide and 4cm (1½in) high

Preheat the oven to 180°C (350°F), Gas Mark 4. Oil the pie dish.

Put the peaches cut-side down evenly over the base of the prepared pie dish. In a bowl, whisk the eggs, yolks, vanilla and caster sugar together until it becomes frothy. Add the flour and salt, then gradually add the double and soured cream and the amaretto, whisking all the time until well combined.

Pour the batter over the fruit and bake in the oven for about 30–35 minutes, possibly a little longer. The fruit should be nicely softened and the mixture set. Remove from the oven and dust with icing sugar. Serve straightaway with some vanilla ice cream – wonderful comfort food.

Spiced blackberry, quince & apple
Pavlova

An autumnal take on the classic Australian pavlova, best served with a glass of good red wine. Quince is a difficult fruit to get hold of, but if you can find it, it makes a sublime addition. Otherwise you could use pears, and you could try raspberries instead of blackberries. Serves 6–8 *(V)*

Meringue

230g (8¼oz) caster sugar

Squeeze of lemon juice

4 egg whites, at room temperature

Fruit filling

3 quince or 4 pears, peeled, cored and sliced

2 apples, peeled, cored and sliced

2 star anise

1 cinnamon stick, snapped in half

Couple of twists of black pepper

½ bottle of Marsala or good red wine

Finely grated zest and juice of 1 orange

4 tbsp soft light brown sugar

seeds of 1 vanilla pod, (save a third of the seeds for the cream filling), or 4 drops of vanilla extract

2 large handfuls of blackberries

▼

Preheat the oven to 140°C (275°F), Gas Mark 1. Line a large baking tray with baking paper.

Put the sugar and lemon juice in a large bowl. Add one egg white and whisk for a minute – the mixture will look hard, but don't worry. Add another egg white and whisk for a few minutes before adding the remaining whites. Then whisk for 4–5 minutes until the meringue is stiff and shiny.

Dollop the mixture in a circle on the baking paper about 20cm (8in) round, making the sides slightly higher than the centre. Bake in the bottom of the oven for 1–1½ hours, or until the meringue is firm and crisp on the outside but still soft and 'pillowy' inside. If you can, wedge the oven door open a tiny bit with a damp tea towel; this allows the moisture to escape and dries out your meringue more quickly. You don't want too much colour – it may begin to turn a very, very pale beige, but that is it. Once cooked, turn off the oven and leave the meringue inside until competely cool.

Meanwhile, put all the fruit filling ingredients except the blackberries in a medium saucepan set over a medium heat. You can throw the vanilla seeds and the pod into the mix. Bring the liquid to just boiling point, then turn down to a poach. (A poach is when there is only one or two bubbles breaking the surface of the liquid.) Cook for about 15 minutes, until the fruit is soft but still has a bit of bite. Add the blackberries and remove the pan from the heat, leaving the fruit to cool in the liquid.

▶

Cream filling

300ml (11fl oz) whipping or double cream

20g (¾oz) icing sugar

a few seeds from vanilla pod (saved from above) or 1 drop vanilla extract

To make the cream filling, put the cream, sugar and vanilla into a large bowl and whip. The cream is whipped enough when it just starts to hold its shape in the bowl and does not run when the bowl is tipped. It is best to very slightly underwhip, as the cream will thicken when left to stand.

Drain the fruit through a sieve or colander, reserving the liquid if you want, to have as a hot toddy.

To assemble the pavlova, place the meringue on a serving plate. Dollop the cream mixture all over it, leaving a 4cm (1½in) border all the way around. Pile the drained fruit all over the cream and serve.

Rum Babas
with star anise cream

Babas are a curious thing. They are not often seen these days, though are still sometimes served with afternoon tea in grand hotels. For a variation, substitute the rum for an orange liqueur and add a bit of orange zest. They taste positively blissful. *Serves 6 (V)*

Rum babas

Vegetable oil, for oiling

310g (11oz) plain flour

½ tsp salt

2 x 14g sachets of fast-action dried yeast

2 big squidges of honey

2 tbsp dark Barbados rum

100ml (4fl oz) single cream

3 egg yolks

115g (4oz) butter, melted

Star anise cream

5 star anise

150ml (5fl oz) whipping cream

2 tbsp icing sugar

Rum soaking syrup

140g (5oz) soft light brown sugar

100ml (4fl oz) water

100ml (4fl oz) dark rum

An empty vanilla pod or 2 drops of vanilla extract

▼

To make the star anise cream, crush the star anise roughly with a pestle and mortar, or put them in a mug and crush with the end of a rolling pin. This is a great opportunity to rid oneself of angst. Place in a small pan, add the cream and heat gently until it is just about to boil, then remove the pan from the heat and set aside for the flavours to steep.

Preheat the oven to 200°C (400°F), Gas Mark 6. Oil the rum baba moulds.

For the rum babas, put the flour, salt and yeast in a large bowl. In a measuring jug, mix the honey, rum, cream, egg yolks and butter together. Make a hole in the centre of the flour mix and pour the honey liquid mixture into it. Beat hard with a wooden spoon for 3–4 minutes. Divide the mixture equally among the prepared baba moulds. For a smooth even top, roll each piece into a ball and put it into the mould. The moulds should feel kind of alien in its nature. It slips and slides between your hands but doesn't stick to them. Loosely cover the babas with oiled clingfilm and leave in a warm place, such as an airing cupboard or the residual heat of an oven, until the mixture has doubled in size.

Bake in the oven for 20–25 minutes, or until the babas have risen nicely and are golden brown.

Meanwhile, make the syrup. Put all the ingredients in a pan and heat gently until the sugar has dissolved, then turn up the heat and boil for 2 minutes.

▶

Rum babas with star anise cream *(cont.)*

Equipment

14 mini rum baba moulds, about 5cm (2in) high, 5cm (2in) across the top and 4cm (1½in) across base

Once the babas are cooked, remove from the oven and leave to cool for 5 minutes before removing them from the moulds. Using a skewer, prick 5 holes in the top of each one then pour over some sugar syrup so the babas are well soaked and syrupy. It is important to do this while the babas are still nice and hot, as the dough will drink up the soaking liquid more readily. Once all the babas have been soaked, make the cream.

Strain the star anise out of the cream through a sieve into a small bowl, then add the icing sugar and whisk until the cream begins to thicken slightly.

Serve the individual babas on small plates with a little dollop of the star anise cream and some more syrup.

Treacle Tart

Good, old-fashioned and truly scrumptious British fare.
Serves 8 *(V)*

1 quantity of sweet shortcrust pastry (see page 220) or 500g (1lb 2oz) shop-bought sweet shortcrust pastry

450g (1lb) golden syrup

Finely grated zest and juice of 1 large lemon

60g (2½oz) butter

1 tsp ground ginger

250g (9oz) breadcrumbs

Equipment

23cm (9in) loose-bottomed tart tin

Preheat the oven to 180°C (350°F), Gas Mark 4. Roll out the pastry on a lightly floured surface to about 3mm (⅛in) thick and use to line the tart tin. Prick the base lightly with a fork and put in the fridge for 20 minutes to firm up.

Once the pastry case is firm, remove it from the fridge. Take a piece of baking paper slightly larger than the tin and scrunch it up, then unscrunch it and place it in the lined tin, taking it right up the sides. Fill it with baking beans or dried beans and 'blind bake' in the oven for 15–20 minutes, until the edges are lightly coloured and the base is dry to the touch. Remove the baking beans and baking paper and return the pastry to the oven for 5 minutes, until golden. Set aside.

To make the filling, put the golden syrup, lemon zest and juice, butter and ground ginger into a large pan and melt gently over a low heat. Stir in the breadcrumbs, then pour the mixture into the pastry case and bake for 20–25 minutes, or until lightly browned and set.

Serve hot or cold with vanilla ice cream or crème anglaise.

White chocolate
Pannacotta

An Italian specialty with a name that means 'cooked cream'. My version also contains mascarpone, however, which gives it a much deeper, richer and naughtier flavour. I like to serve it with raspberries and ginger brittle. Serves 4

Vegetable oil, for oiling

4 leaves of gelatine (check on the packet how much is needed to set 600ml/1 pint liquid, as different brands vary)

300ml (11fl oz) double cream

1 x 250g (9oz) tub of mascarpone or fresh brillat savarin cheese

Seeds of 1 vanilla pod or 2 drops of vanilla extract

100g (3½oz) good white chocolate (at least 30% cocoa solids or more), grated

200g (7oz or 1 punnet) raspberries

Ginger brittle

80g (3oz) granulated sugar

2 tbsp water

1 tiny drop of peppermint essence

4cm (1½in) piece of fresh ginger, peeled and grated

Equipment

4 dariole moulds

Thoroughly oil the dariole moulds and a large baking tray.

Put the gelatine leaves in a bowl of cold water, making sure they are fully covered, and set aside for 5 minutes.

Put the double cream, mascarpone and vanilla in a pan and stir to combine. Heat the mixture gently so it is hot but not boiling, then remove the pan from the heat. Add the grated chocolate and leave it to melt for 2 minutes, then stir to combine.

Pick up the gelatine leaves – they should be completely softened by now – and squeeze out all the water. Place them into the warmed cream mixture and stir gently until all the gelatine has dissolved. Put a sieve over a jug and pour the mixture through it to get rid of any bits. Now pour the sieved mixture into the dariole moulds and leave to cool. Once cooled, place in the fridge for 2–3 hours to set.

Meanwhile, to make the brittle, put the sugar and water in a small pan over a low heat and heat gently until the sugar has dissolved. Once the liquid has turned clear, turn up the heat and boil; the bubbles will get bigger and the sugary water will begin to turn brown at the edges. Do not stir it at this point but swirl the pan around to mix in any darker bits around the edges. After a couple of minutes the whole mixture will begin to go a light brown, now add the peppermint essence and grated ginger, swirling the pan around. When the mixture goes a honeycomb colour, cook for a further 1 minute, then pour it onto the oiled baking tray and leave for a few minutes to cool and harden. Set aside.

▶

White chocolate pannacotta *(cont.)*

Once the pannacotta are set, remove them from the fridge. The easiest way to unmould them is by dipping the bottom of the dariole moulds in some hot water for a couple of seconds, then turning them upside down onto the serving plate. They may need a few sharp jerks of the hand for them to come out. If this fails, run a small knife all around the side of the mould to loosen it slightly.

Sprinkle the raspberries on the top of the pannacottas. The brittle is for decoration and it can be broken into shards with one piece laid against the pannacotta or whizzed in the blender to a rough powder and sprinkled on the plate. Either way you will have a restaurant-style dessert on the plate.

Apple, chestnut & rosemary
Galette

A good entry-level tart if you're not yet entirely confident with lining pastry tins and the like. This free-form tart allows you to be creative because you can shape it just the way you want it. Release your inner artiste. Serves 6–8 *(V)*

1 quantity of sweet shortcrust pastry (see page 220) or 300g (10½oz) shop-bought shortcrust pastry

Plain flour, for dusting

25g (1oz) butter

80g (3oz) soft light brown sugar, plus 3 tbsp to sprinkle

3 eating apples, peeled, cored and sliced into eighths

80g (3oz) chestnuts (tinned is fine), roughly chopped

Small handful of rosemary leaves, finely chopped

1 egg, lightly beaten

60g (2½oz) white breadcrumbs

Preheat the oven to 190°C (375°F), Gas Mark 5.

If using homemade pastry, make it according to the recipe on page 220. Roll out the pastry on a lightly floured work surface to a 30cm (12in) circle, then transfer to a baking tray and put it in the fridge for about 30 minutes, or until firm.

Melt the butter and 80g (3oz) of the sugar in a sauté pan, then add the apples. Keep them moving around in the pan until they start to go brown and begin to caramelise. Add the chestnuts and rosemary and cook for 2 more minutes, then remove the pan from the heat and set aside.

Remove the pastry from the fridge and let it soften for 2 minutes. Brush a 4cm (1½in) border with the egg, then sprinkle inside the border with the breadcrumbs and 1 tablespoon of sugar. Layer the apple mix on top of the breadcrumbs, sprinkle over another tablespoon of sugar and fold the 4cm (1½in) border in to cover the edge of the fruit. The breadcrumbs will help soak up some of the fruit's juices so the bottom of the galette is not too soggy. I try to do the folding as neatly as possible but the rustic look is good for this dish. Brush the folded over edge with some more egg. Sprinkle the top of the pastry with the remaining sugar and bake in the oven for 25 minutes. The galette is ready when the apples are softened and the pastry is turning golden brown.

Leave to cool for 30 minutes before serving. Best served with a dollop of fresh whipped cream and a glass of a full-bodied red wine.

The Skinny Tart

So there's a smidgeon of butter on, and in, the pastry, but otherwise these fruity little minxes are a rare guilt-free treat and if you get a wriggle on they can be made in under an hour. Impeccable. *Makes 8 tarts (V)*

80g (3oz) butter, melted and cooled, plus extra for greasing

270g (10oz) shop-bought filo pastry

4 tbsp apricot jam

500g (1lb 2oz) low- or no-fat Greek yoghurt

2 tbsp honey

Seeds of 1 vanilla pod or 2 drops of vanilla extract

Small bunch of black seedless grapes, halved

Bunch of redcurrants

1 dragon fruit, peeled and cubed

2 large figs, quartered

Equipment

12-hole muffin tin or cupcake tin

Preheat the oven to 180°C (350°F), Gas Mark 4 with the middle shelf ready. Grease the muffin or cupcake tin well.

Cut the filo pastry into squares that are big enough to fit into the muffin holes and hang over the sides a little. Brush each piece of filo with lots of melted butter to stop them from burning in the oven, then push a filo square into a hole and add another filo square, you will need to layer up 3–4 pieces. Repeat until you have 8 holes filled.

Place the filo cases into the oven for 5 minutes or so, giving them time to crisp up. Once they look golden brown and crispy remove them from the oven and leave to cool for 10 minutes or so. Remove them from the muffin tray and place them on serving dishes. I always tend to break at least one when I take them out!

Put the jam in a small pan and heat gently until warm.

Mix the Greek yoghurt, honey and vanilla together in a bowl then place a good dollop into each pastry case. Now divide the fruit among the tartlets, piling it up high. Brush with the warm apricot jam to make a shiny glaze and serve. You can make all the component parts ahead of time and assemble the tarts at the last minute.

You can also decorate with a sprig of fresh mint, or get creative with some raspberry jam thinned and well mixed with some water and drizzle it on the plate for a touch of old-school food glamour.

Ginger, rhubarb & blueberry
Crumble

Turn classic British crumble into a dinner-party dish by baking it in individual ramekins.
Serves 6 (V)

200g (7oz or 1 punnet) blueberries

150ml (5fl oz) water

150g (5oz) granulated sugar

About 20 sticks of rhubarb, cut into 4cm (1½in) pieces

1cm (½in) piece of fresh grated ginger

Finely grated zest of ½ lemon

Crumble topping

200g (7oz) plain flour

Pinch of salt

Pinch of ground cinnamon

115g (4oz) cold butter, cut into pieces

80g (3oz) granulated sugar

Equipment

Large casserole dish

Preheat the oven to 200°C (400°F), Gas Mark 6, and put the middle shelf in position. Spread the blueberries over the base of the casserole dish.

Put the water and sugar in a pan over a medium heat and let the sugar dissolve. Add the rhubarb and ginger, reduce the heat to very low and cook until the rhubarb just starts to soften. Remove the pan from the heat.

To make the crumble topping, put the flour, salt, cinnamon and butter into a food processor and mix until you have fine breadcrumbs. The trick is not to overmix it otherwise the mixture turns into one big clump, which means the crumble will not be crumbly! If not using a food processor, put the flour, salt, cinnamon and butter in a large bowl and, using your fingers, rub together until the mixture resembles fine breadcrumbs. Add the sugar and blitz briefly again or mix in.

Drain the rhubarb in a sieve or colander over a bowl, reserving the juice that drips through. Allow to drain for a few minutes, as too much liquid in the fruit will result in soggy crumble. Then spread the rhubarb on top of the blueberries. The reserved juice is delicious and can be kept in the fridge for 3–4 weeks and used in fruit salads, etc. Sprinkle the lemon zest over the rhubarb, then pile the crumble topping all over the fruit. Bake in the oven for 35–45 minutes, or until the topping goes brown and crunchy.

Serve with a dollop of mascarpone, crème anglaise or ready-made custard. To turn this into a dinner party dish, make the crumble in individual ramekins.

Banana & honey
Soufflé

Quick to prepare and really tasty, this is a great one to knock up when speed is of the essence. Try this when you want something a bit cosy and special for an afternoon treat or an autumnal dinner party. Use ripe bananas if possible, as they have a sweeter flavour and soft texture. Serves 4 *(V)*

30g (1oz) butter, softened for greasing

100g (3½oz) caster sugar

2 large or 3 small ripe bananas

1 tbsp honey

Seeds of ½ vanilla pod or 2 drops of vanilla extract

Large pinch of finely grated lemon zest

4 egg whites

Hot Chocolate Sauce (see page 172), to serve

Equipment

4 large ramekins, about 350ml (12fl oz) capacity

Preheat the oven to 200°C (400°F), Gas Mark 6. Put a baking tray in the oven, large enough to hold the ramekins, and grease the ramekins with the softened butter, using a pastry brush with upward strokes. Put 40g (1½oz) of the caster sugar in the ramekins and tilt and turn them so that the sugar sticks to the butter. This gives the soft soufflé a crunchy outer shell. Tip out the excess sugar.

Put the bananas, honey, vanilla and lemon zest in a blender and whiz to a smooth purée, then spoon into a large bowl.

Whisk the egg whites in a clean bowl until they begin to form soft peaks, then gradually add the remaining caster sugar and whisk until medium-stiff peaks form. Stir a spoonful of the meringue into the banana purée to thin it out a little, then add the rest of the meringue to the purée mix. Using a metal spoon or large plastic spatula, slowly fold the two mixtures together, keeping in as much air as possible.

Divide the mixture among the prepared ramekins, filling them right to the top, then bang them a couple of times on a work surface to make sure the mixture goes right into the edges, allowing for a more even rise. Run a palette knife across the top of each soufflé so it is completely level, and run your thumb all the way around the edge to make sure that none of the mixture sticks to the ramekin, as this prevents a high rise.

Remove the baking tray from the oven and arrange the ramekins on it. Bake for 8–10 minutes. The soufflés should be well risen, but still a bit *baveuse,* or runny, in the middle. Serve immediately. To be superflash, make a hole in the middle of each soufflé and pour in some hot chocolate sauce, or serve the sauce on the side.

Lemon & Raspberry
tart with poppy seed pastry

Lemon and raspberry is one of my favourite flavour combinations. The poppy seeds give the tender pastry crust a sensational crunch. If your make-your-own-pastry-phobia has not yet gone, use a pack of shop-bought sweet shortcrust pastry instead (I promise I won't judge). Serves 8 (V)

Poppy seed pastry

100g (3½oz) butter, softened

100g (3½oz) caster sugar

Seeds from ½ vanilla pod or 2 drops of vanilla extract

3 egg yolks

200g (7oz) plain flour, plus extra for dusting

Pinch of salt

2 tbsp poppy seeds

1 egg, lightly beaten

Filling

4 eggs

200g (7oz) caster sugar

165ml (5½fl oz) whipping or double cream

Juice and finely grated zest of 5 lemons

Topping

300g (10½oz) raspberries

Icing sugar, to dust

Equipment

20cm (8in) loose-bottomed tart tin, about 5cm (2in) deep

To make the pastry, put the butter, sugar and vanilla in a large bowl and beat until creamy. Beat in the egg yolks one at a time, then sift in the flour and salt. Add the poppy seeds and stir together gently to make a soft, uniform dough. Shape into a ball. Wrap in clingfilm and put in the fridge for about 2 hours, or until firm.

Once the dough has firmed up, remove it from the fridge and leave at room temperature for 5 minutes, then roll out on a floured work surface to about 3mm (⅛in) thick. Lay it over the tart tin and push it gently into the corners to ensure lovely straight edges when the tart comes out of the tin. The easiest way to do this is to take a small ball of pastry (the size of a £1 coin) and use it to gently ease the dough into the corners. If the pastry case breaks, as it may, just patch it up with an odd bit of pastry. Don't stretch or pull the pastry (which often seems like the only way to line a tin), or your tart case will shrink in the oven. Guiding and coaxing will yield the best results! If you find the dough getting too soft, then just pop back in the fridge for 15 minutes to harden up. Trim off the excess pastry about 2cm (¾in) above the top of the tin using a sharp knife. Put the tart case in the fridge for about 30 minutes to firm up.

Preheat the oven to 180°C (350°F), Gas Mark 4.

Remove the tin from the fridge. Take a piece of baking paper slightly larger than the tart and scrunch it up, then unscrunch it and line the tart with it, taking it right up the sides. Fill it with baking beans or dried beans and 'blind bake' in the oven for 20 minutes, or until the pastry begins to feel firm. Remove the baking beans and paper and cook for a

▶

Lemon and raspberry tart with poppy seed pastry *(cont.)*

further 5 minutes. There should be no colour on the tart when it is cooked but the base will feel slightly sandy and the sides will have firmed up.

Turn the oven down to 160°C (315°F), Gas Mark 3.

Now make the filling. Put the eggs and sugar in a large bowl and whisk together gently. Add the cream and whisk for a couple of minutes, then stir in the lemon zest and juice. Pour the mixture into the tart case until it is almost full and bake in the oven for 40–45 minutes, or until the lemon mixture is set but still has a very slight wobble in the centre.

Leave the tart to cool, then decorate the top with raspberries and sprinkle with icing sugar. Serve with single cream.

Lime & ginger
Posset

It's easy to set the bar too high when cooking for a dinner party, choosing ambitious starters and main courses that take all day to prepare. To counterbalance such culinary extravagance, your pudding should be simple, like this mouth-watering posset, which takes only moments to prepare. Serves 6 (V)

500ml (18fl oz) whipping cream

60g (2½oz) stem ginger syrup

½ knob of stem ginger, finely grated

Seeds of 1 vanilla pod or 2 drops of vanilla extract

Finely grated zest of 2–3 limes

Lime juice, to taste

Equipment

6 Martini or Champagne glasses

Whip the cream in a large bowl until it begins to thicken. Stir in the ginger syrup, grated stem ginger, vanilla, lime zest and juice to taste. Spoon into 4 glasses and put in the fridge for at least an hour.

Serve with fresh raspberries or blueberries and shortbread, preferably stem ginger shortbread (see page 195).

Simple!

Rosewater & walnut
Vanilla Fool

Trousers feeling a little on the tight side? Make this fool 100 per cent healthy by replacing the cream with Greek yoghurt for a quick and guilt-free dessert. Serves 4 *(V)*

350ml (12fl oz) whipping cream

3 tbsp icing sugar

Seeds of 1 vanilla pod or 2 drops of vanilla extract

150ml (5fl oz) Greek yoghurt

2 drops of rosewater

Squeeze of lime juice

Large handful of roughly chopped walnuts, plus extra to decorate

Fresh mint, to decorate (optional)

Equipment

4 large Martini glasses or ramekins

Put the cream, icing sugar and vanilla in a large bowl and whip until it begins to thicken. Fold in the Greek yoghurt, rosewater and lime juice, followed by the walnuts.

Spoon the mixture into the serving glasses and place in the fridge to chill for at least 30 minutes.

Once ready, remove the glasses from the fridge, sprinkle over some roughly chopped walnuts, decorate with mint and, if you like, serve with crisp biscuits or shortbread.

Sticky toffee
Pudding

This pudding recipe is for individual portions, but it can also be baked in a square or rectangular tin. If so, the cooking time may need to be adjusted, depending on the size of baking tin used. Serves 6 *(V)*

150g (5oz) butter, softened, plus extra for greasing

200g (7oz) soft light brown sugar, plus extra for coating

165g (5½oz) medjool dates, stoned and finely chopped

1 small bowl of builder's tea (you need enough to cover the dates)

Seeds of ½ vanilla pod or 2 drops of vanilla extract

4 eggs

260g (9oz) plain flour

Pinch of salt

1 tbsp baking powder

½ tsp bicarbonate of soda

Sauce

100g (3½oz) butter

110g (4oz) soft light brown sugar

3 tbsp whipping cream

Seeds from ½ vanilla pod or 2 drops of vanilla extract

Equipment

Six timbale moulds, about 9 x 5 x 4.5cm (3½ x 2 x 1¾in)

Place a roasting tin full of water on the bottom of the oven to create a steamy environment for the puds. Preheat the oven to 180°C (350°F), Gas Mark 4. Grease the timbale moulds and coat them with sugar (see page 115).

Put the dates and tea into a small pan and heat to below boiling point, then remove the pan from the heat and leave to steep for 10 minutes.

Put the butter, sugar and vanilla in a large bowl and cream together until pale and fluffy. Add two eggs and roughly half of the flour and mix well. Add the other two eggs and the rest of the flour together with the salt, baking powder and bicarbonate of soda and beat until combined.

Drain the dates from the tea mixture and stir them into the cake batter. Divide the mixture equally among the moulds. The cake batter should come two-thirds up the side of the moulds. Bake in the oven for 30–35 minutes. The cake should come away from the sides of the moulds slightly and the sponge will be nice and bouncy on the top.

To make the sauce, put the butter and sugar in a pan and melt together over a low heat. Add the cream and vanilla, then turn up the heat and boil for 2–3 minutes until it begins to thicken. Remove the pan from the heat.

To serve, unmould the puds and plop straight onto serving plates. Pour the hot toffee sauce over them and serve immediately with some vanilla ice cream.

Les petits
Croquembouches

Choux pastry is traditionally made with water, but here buttermilk is substituted, which helps to keep the buns light and tender. Serves 4–6 (V)

Choux pastry

70g (3oz) plain flour, plus extra for dusting

60g (2½oz) butter

150ml (5fl oz) buttermilk, or milk plus a squeeze of lemon juice

Pinch of salt

2–3 eggs

Coffee and vanilla cream

200ml (7fl oz) whipping cream or double cream

40g (1½oz) icing sugar

Seeds of ½ vanilla pod or 2 drops of vanilla extract

1 tbsp instant coffee powder, few drops of coffee essence or 1 tbsp Irish cream liqueur

Spun sugar

165g (5½oz) granulated sugar

165ml (5½fl oz) water

Equipment

Piping bag fitted with a small round piping nozzle

Preheat the oven to 180°C (350°F), Gas Mark 4. Dust a large baking tray with flour.

To make the pastry, put the butter and buttermilk in a medium pan set over a low heat and let the butter melt. Once the butter has completely melted turn the liquid up to a fast boil. Add the flour and salt quickly in one go, then remove the pan from the heat stirring all the time. Beat hard until the mixture leaves the sides of the pan then set aside to cool to body temperature.

Meanwhile, to make the cream, whip the cream, icing sugar and vanilla together in a large bowl until it begins to thicken. Stir in the coffee and set aside. The cream will continue to thicken as it sits in the bowl so underwhip it slightly.

Add the eggs to the choux pastry mixture, one by one, beating really hard after each addition. It is tempting to add the eggs all at once but then they will not all be absorbed into the flour mix. When the first egg is added it will seem as if the mixture has become too watery but keep beating it and it will go thick again. You will notice the mixture goes shiny and begins to come away from the sides of the pan. The correct consistency should fall slowly from a spoon after a slight jerk of the wrist. It should plop down slowly and reluctantly. You may not need all the eggs, I usually use 2½ eggs.

Put the choux dough in a piping bag fitted with a small round piping nozzle and pipe tiny buns 2cm (¾in) high, 3cm (1¼in) wide and about

▶

Les petits croquembouches *(cont.)*

3cm (1¼in) apart onto the prepared baking tray. Pipe until you have used up all of the mixture. Bake in the oven for about 20 minutes. Keep an eye on your buns, as the cooking time depends so much on what size you have piped them. Once the buns have puffed up nicely, are firm around the edge and a light golden brown, remove them from the oven. Using a skewer make a hole about 1cm (0.5in) in diameter in the underside of each bun. Place them back in the oven for a couple of minutes to dry out the inside. Leave the buns to cool on a wire rack.

To assemble, put a dollop of the coffee and vanilla cream on a serving plate and arrange a few buns on it. Put a smaller dollop on top of that layer and fill it with buns. Repeat until you have a three-layered structure.

To make the spun sugar, have a large flat-bottomed bowl or large sauté pan of cold water ready, this will stop the caramel cooking once it has reached the correct temperature. Put the sugar and water in a heavy-based saucepan and melt over a low heat. If any bits of sugar look like they are beginning to burn on the sides of the pan use a pastry brush to brush down the sides of the pan. Once the sugar has completely dissolved, turn up the heat and let it boil and bubble gently until it begins to go a medium honeycomb colour. As soon as it reaches this stage, plunge the bottom of the pan into the bowl of cold water.

For the sugared finish, using two forks back to back, dunk them in the sugar so there is a good amount on them and spin the sugar round and round the croquembouche, about 10–15 times, forming a sugar 'net' around the choux buns.

The sugar net will hold for an hour or two, so making it a great dessert to serve at a dinner party and giving you time to enjoy your guests!

White chocolate & amaretti
Cheesecake

Quick and easy, amaretti squeasy; a no-cook dessert which, though not baked, tastes too good to be left out. Make ahead of time to lessen the pre-dinner-party stress factor. Serves 8–10 (V)

Biscuit base

165g (5½oz) digestive biscuits, crushed

60g (2½oz) amaretti biscuits, crushed

80g (3oz) butter

Filling

1 x 250g (9oz) tub of mascarpone

1 tbsp amaretto liqueur

300ml (11fl oz) whipping cream

300g (10½oz) white chocolate, melted (see page 45)

Equipment

20cm (8in) springform cake tin

To make the biscuit base, mix the digestive and the amaretti biscuits together in a bowl. Reserve a handful for the topping at the end. Melt the butter in a small pan over a medium heat. Once it is melted, turn up the heat slightly and cook until small specks of brown appear in the butter and it begins to have a nutty smell. Pour the butter into the biscuits and mix together well. Press this mixture into the base of the tin and flatten well. Put in the fridge to set.

For the filling, beat the mascarpone until smooth, then beat in the Amaretto. In a separate bowl, whip the cream until it forms soft peaks. Stir a little of the cream into the mascarpone mixture to loosen it, then fold this mixture into the remaining cream. Gently mix in the melted white chocolate.

Remove the biscuit base from the fridge and spoon over the white chocolate mix. Return to the fridge for 1 hour or until set.

When ready to serve, remove the cheesecake from the tin and place on a serving plate. Sprinkle over the reserved crushed biscuits and serve.

Dinner
Party

I threw my first dinner party when I was in my early twenties.
The menu was much too ambitious, requiring a shopping
list as long as my arm and the whole of the previous night
spent cooking. By the time my guests arrived, I was far too
frazzled to enjoy their company, let alone the food. Thankfully,
nearly all the dishes in this chapter are relatively effortless
to make, with just a couple of dishes, like the aristocratic
Charlotte Russe and the glacial Baked Alaska, requiring
a touch more application.

*'My doctor has told me to stop having
intimate dinners for four unless there are
three other people involved.'*

Orson Welles
Actor, Director, Producer, Screenwriter
1915 – 1985

Parmesan & poppy seed
Lollipops

Put away those toasted nuts and crisps! Canapés have reached a whole new dimension. Makes 10 lollipops

Butter, for greasing

80g (3oz) Parmesan cheese, finely grated

1 tsp poppy seeds

1 tsp sesame seeds

Equipment

10 white round lollipop sticks

Round 9cm (3½in) cookie cutter

2 baking trays

Preheat the oven to 220°C (425°F), Gas Mark 7. Line two large baking trays with baking paper and grease.

Toss the cheese and seeds together in a small bowl. Sit a 9cm (3½in) ring or cookie cutter on one of the baking trays and sprinkle a small handful of the cheese mixture into it, in a thin layer. Carefully lift the ring off to reveal a neat-edged disc of Parmesan and lay a lollipop stick on top, with the tip of the stick touching the middle of the disc. Repeat with the remaining cheese and sticks to make 10 in total (leaving about 3cm (1¼in) spaces between them to allow for any spreading during cooking).

You should have a little Parmesan left over, so use it to cover up the part of the lollipop stick resting on the disc.

Bake in the oven for 5 minutes, swapping to a different shelf halfway through. The cheese should be lightly golden and bubbling.

Remove from the oven and slide the paper off the baking trays and onto a rack to help speed up cooling. Leave to cool for 1–2 minutes until the lollipops have become crisp. Very carefully remove each one with a palette knife. I like to serve these stuck upright into a box with holes in the top.

Sun-dried tomato & rosemary
Palmiers

Super-quick canapés or an easy picnic snack. Makes 25–30 (V)

1 quantity of puff pastry
(see page 218) or 500g
(1lb 2oz) shop-bought
puff pastry

Plain flour, for dusting

1 x 280g (10oz) jar of
sun-dried tomatoes, drained
and finely chopped

Few sprigs of fresh
rosemary, leaves only, finely
chopped

1 egg, lightly beaten

If using homemade pastry, make it according to the recipe on page 218. Put the puff pastry on a well-floured surface and bash it with a rolling pin. Usually we need to be quite delicate with puff pastry as it needs to puff up a lot, but for palmiers it only needs to puff up a little. Roll the pastry out into a rectangle about 30 x 35cm (12 x 14in) and the thickness of a £1 coin. Spread the tomatoes over the puff pastry and sprinkle over the rosemary.

With the shortest end facing you, take both long edges of the pastry and roll them towards each other to meet in the middle. Brush a little egg down the centre to stick the two halves together. Carefully lift into a large baking tray, making sure it will fit in your fridge first, and put in the fridge for at least 30 minutes to chill and harden.

Preheat the oven to 200°C (400°F), Gas Mark 6.

Remove the roll from the fridge and, using a very sharp knife, slice it into 1cm (½in) thick pieces. Lay each piece on the baking tray and brush well with the beaten egg then bake in the oven for 10–15 minutes until puffed up, crisp and golden.

Remove the palmiers from the oven and leave to cool on the baking tray. To serve, pile them high on a plate. These are great little canapés for waiting guests.

Feta, pomegranate & mint
Vol-au-vents

When was the last time you had a vol-au-vent? Those under the age of 30 are probably wondering what on earth I'm talking about. We do not see enough of these retro beauties anymore. Bring back the vol-au-vent! Makes 8 vol-au-vents (V)

Handful of pine nuts

1 quantity of puff pastry (see page 218) or 500g (1lb 2oz) shop-bought puff pastry

Plain flour, for dusting

1 egg, lightly beaten

200g (7oz) feta cheese

Freshly ground black pepper

1 pomegranate, seeds and juice separated

1 large bunch of fresh mint, ripped

Equipment

5.5cm (2¼in) cutter

Preheat the oven to 200°C (400°F), Gas Mark 6. Put the pine nuts in a dry frying pan and toast gently. Remove from the heat and set aside.

If using homemade pastry, follow the recipe on page 218. Roll out the pastry on a well-floured work surface to the thickness of a £1 coin. Cut out 8 rounds, about 8cm (3in) wide, and put on a baking tray. Coffee mugs and glasses make good templates for the circles.

Don't scrunch up the pastry trimmings (or they won't puff up), but put the bits on top of each other and roll out again. For the vol-au-vent tops, cut out 8 more circles, then use the 5.5cm (2¼in) cutter to cut a smaller circle from inside each bigger circle. Discard the smaller circles or keep for something else. Use the ring for the tops of the pastries. Brush the original 8 rounds with lightly beaten egg, then place a ring on top of each and also brush this with egg, making sure it does not drip down the sides. Place the vol-au-vents in the fridge for about 30 minutes, or until firm.

Remove the vol-au-vents from the fridge and bake in the oven for 15–20 minutes, or until the pastry is firm, well risen and a rich golden brown. Remove from the oven and leave to cool.

For the filling, mix the feta and toasted pine nuts in a bowl and season with freshly ground black pepper. Fill the cooled pastries with the mixture, then sprinkle pomegranate seeds and ripped mint leaves over the top. (If you are making these ahead of time, add the filling to the vol-au-vents at the last minute, or the pomegranate seeds will dye the feta cheese pink!)

Serve as part of a buffet with delights such as pineapple on sticks, cheese hedgehogs and a sparking glass of Baby Cham.

Gorgonzola & pear
Soufflé

The elegant soufflé is often perceived as off-limits, even for cooks with experience. However, this needn't be your Achilles heel. Mightily impressive to serve and gorgeous to eat, soufflés are a wonder of modern cooking alchemy – in short, they're a little bit of culinary magic. Practise a few times to get it perfect, and I guarantee it will become a firm favourite. If you prefer a milder flavour, you can replace the gorgonzola with a good English Cheddar. Serves 8 for a starter and 4 as a main *(V if veggie cheese used)*

2 medium pears, peeled, cored and cut into large chunks

150ml (5fl oz) port

Salt and freshly ground black pepper

40g (1½oz) unsalted butter, plus 2 tsp for greasing

75g (3oz) breadcrumbs

40g (1½oz) plain flour

150ml (5fl oz) milk

75g (3oz) Gorgonzola cheese

1 tsp mustard powder

5 eggs, separated

Squeeze of lemon juice

Equipment

1 large soufflé dish, 4 soufflé dishes or 8 ramekins

Put the pears in a pan with the port, black pepper and enough water to cover the pears. Bring to just under the boil and then turn down the heat so only a couple of bubbles break the surface of the liquid. Continue cooking until the pears are just beginning to go soft, then remove the pan from the heat and leave the pears to infuse for a few minutes.

Preheat the oven to 200°C (400°F), Gas Mark 6 and place a baking tray in the oven. For a really good soufflé you need direct bottom heat, as this will give the eggs a good upward boost in the oven.

Prepare 1 large soufflé dish, 4 soufflé dishes or I used ramekins. Butter the sides of the ramekins really well then tip some breadcrumbs into each mould and turn the ramekins around so that the breadcrumbs stick to the butter. Pour out the excess breadcrumbs. The breadcrumbs will give the soufflé a crispy crunchy crust.

Remove the pears from the port and cut them into bite-sized cubes, then put them in the soufflé dish or divide them equally among the individual dishes.

Heat the butter in a medium pan over a low heat, add the flour and stir to combine well. Remove the pan from the heat and gradually add the milk, bit by bit, stirring all the time. If it goes in all at once the mix will be lumpy, so start with a little and then keep adding and stirring lots. If you find it has gone lumpy, all is not lost. Just whisk it like mad to get rid of all the lumps.

▶

Turn up the heat until the mixture is boiling and cook for a further 2–3 minutes – the sauce will begin to thicken. Remove the pan from the heat and add the Gorgonzola, mustard and season to taste with salt and pepper. This mix (called the panade) will need more seasoning than usual as the eggs dilute the strength of the flavour somewhat. Now add the egg yolks and stir well.

Put the egg whites and a squeeze of lemon juice in a clean bowl and whisk. Start whisking slowly at first and then pick up speed. The whites should be whisked to a shiny and stiff peak and will hold their shape in the bowl. Add one big spoonful of the whites to the cheese mix and stir. This loosens the mix a little and makes it easier to add the egg whites. Using a large metal spoon, slowly fold in the egg whites keeping as much air in the soufflé as possible.

Remove the hot baking tray from the oven and place the dish or dishes on it, then divide the uncooked soufflé mix among them. Run a finger along the edge of the ramekin so none of the mixture is coming over the side. Then use a palette knife to level the top of the soufflé so it rises evenly. Bake immediately in the oven for 20–25 minutes for the large one and 10 minutes for small ones. It is okay to have a quick peek in the middle of baking – the soufflés will only collapse if they are allowed to cool down. Having said that, opening the oven will bring down the temperature of the oven and your soufflés will not get that rising boost they need, so if you can resist, don't peek!

Once they are ready, remove them from the oven. The soufflé should have a little bit in the middle which is still liquid, or 'baveuse'. They do have a tendency to fall quite rapidly so they really need to go straight from the oven to table! Serve as an impressive starter to set off your dinner party.

Whisky & chilli
Tiger Prawns

This gratifyingly tactile dish is best served as a starter. Sucking the sweet sauce off the juicy crustaceans is an experience to be savoured, never hurried. Shelled and unshelled prawns are both fine to use. I take mine shell on; how do you like yours? Serves 4 as a starter or 2 as a main course

Juice of 2 limes

90ml (3½fl oz) whisky

180g (6½oz) soft light brown sugar

Finely grated zest of 1 lime

20 raw tiger prawns, peeled and deveined (optional)

1 red chilli, deseeded and finely chopped

1 tbsp vegetable oil

Equipment

Shallow ovenproof dish

Preheat the oven to 200°C (400°F), Gas Mark 6.

Put the lime juice, whisky and sugar in a pan over a medium heat and cook, stirring gently, until the sugar has dissolved. Once the sugar has all dissolved, stop stirring, turn up the heat and boil for 5–7 minutes, or until the mixture goes syrupy and thickens. To tell if it is ready, dip a wooden spoon in the mixture and tap off the excess – some glaze should still stick to the spoon, but it will not be as thick as honey. Sometimes the whisky catches alight and you will see a blue-orange flame coming from the pan. Just take it off the heat and the whisky will burn itself out. Stir in the finely grated lime zest, then remove the pan from the heat and set aside.

Put the prawns in a shallow ovenproof dish and sprinkle over the chilli. Brush the prawns with some oil and then with the glaze. Bake in the oven for 10–15 minutes, or until the prawns turn opaque. Remove from the oven and brush with more glaze. Reserve the extra glaze for dipping.

Leave to cool slightly (the glaze gets ridiculously hot) and serve, with a significant other, a huge green salad and hunks of crunchy bread.

Fig, cream cheese & mint
Tart

A real stunner and a snappy one to prepare. Serve with a simple rocket or spinach salad. Serves 8–10 (V)

1 quantity of shortcrust pastry (see page 220) or 500g (1lb 2oz) shop-bought shortcrust pastry

Plain flour, for dusting

260ml (9½fl oz) whipping cream

165g (5½oz) cream cheese

3 big squidges of honey

1 tbsp Marsala (optional)

12–16 figs, each cut into 6 pieces

Handful of green shelled pistachios, walnuts or pecans, halved

1 bunch of fresh mint, ripped or roughly torn

Equipment

20 x 30cm (8 x 12in) rectangular fluted tin

Preheat the oven to 180°C (350°F), Gas Mark 4.

If using homemade pastry, make it according to the recipe on page 220. Roll out the pastry on a floured work surface to the thickness of half a £1 coin and use it to carefully line the tin. Homemade pastry is short and so will be quite crumbly. Don't be alarmed by this, you can patch it together in the tin. Take a small ball of the pastry (the size of a £1 coin) and use it to gently ease the dough down into the tin. Press the handle of a wooden spoon against the pastry all round the edges to coax it into the fluted grooves. Trim off the excess around the top and run a thin knife around between the pastry and the edge of the tin to loosen. Put in the fridge for about 15 minutes, or until firm.

Remove the tart from the fridge. Take a piece of baking paper slightly larger than the tin and scrunch it up, then unscrunch it and line the tin with it. Fill it with baking beans or dried beans and 'blind bake' in the oven for 20–25 minutes, or until the pastry feels sandy to the touch. Remove from the oven and set aside.

For the filling, put the cream in a bowl and whip until beginning to thicken, then fold it into the cream cheese and mix with the honey and Marsala, if using. Put the filling in the tart case, then arrange the figs on top and scatter over the nuts and mint. Serve with a sweet wine such as Asti.

Figs and mint are delicious so sprinkling some torn mint leaves over the tart works really well. This tart is best eaten on the day it is made.

Lemon, thyme & chilli
Scallops

Dainty, elegant and provocative, served on the half scallop shell. Serves 4

12 scallops in their shells

Salt and freshly ground
black pepper

50g (2oz) butter

Finely grated zest of
1 lemon

Small handful of fresh thyme
leaves

1 small red chilli, deseeded
and very finely chopped

Juice of 1 lemon, to serve

Preheat the oven to 180°C (350°F), Gas Mark 4.

Remove the top of the scallops' shells, cut off the roe and discard (this is optional, I prefer mine without). Place the scallops on a baking tray and season with salt and a little pepper. Add a small knob of butter, finely grated lemon zest, a pinch of thyme and chilli to your taste to each scallop.

Bake in the oven for 8 minutes until cooked. Serve on a bed of mixed lettuce leaves, drizzled with some extra-virgin olive oil. Squeeze a little lemon juice over the scallops to serve.

Garlic & sherry
Mussels

The flavours of mussels and sherry go beautifully together. This recipe can be made equally well on the hob. Serves 4 as a main or 8 as a starter

Glug of extra-virgin olive oil

3 shallots, peeled and finely chopped

1 clove of garlic, peeled and finely chopped

300ml (11fl oz) sherry

1 bay leaf

Salt and freshly ground black pepper

2kg (4½lb) live mussels, cleaned and beards removed

1 bunch of fresh flat-leaf parsley, chopped

Equipment

Ovenproof frying pan or casserole dish

Preheat the oven to 200°C (400°F), Gas Mark 6.

Heat the oil in a large ovenproof frying pan, if you have one, add the shallots and fry until the shallots are translucent and soft. Add the garlic and cook for 1 minute, then add the sherry. Turn up the heat and boil for 2–3 minutes. Add the bay leaf and cook for a further 1 minute. Season to taste with salt and pepper.

Add the mussels to the pan. If you don't have an ovenproof frying pan then tip this mixture into a large casserole dish and add the mussels. Cover with a lid or foil and bake in the oven for about 8 minutes, or until the mussels have opened. Remove from the oven and remove and discard any mussels that have not opened.

Divide the mixture among warmed bowls, then sprinkle over the parsley and serve with hunks of crispy bread.

Peppered Beef
with Cognac & Parma-wrapped green beans

Rich, sumptuous comfort food, with a sauce so good you'll want to lick the plate clean. Dress up your accompanying veg by serving these green beans wrapped in slices of salty Parma ham. Serves 4

Few glugs of olive oil

3 shallots, peeled and chopped

Salt and freshly ground black pepper

800g (1¾lb) beef fillet

40g (1½oz) butter

Large handful of cracked black, green and pink peppercorns, or just black if the others are not available

1 tsp Dijon mustard

80ml (3fl oz) Cognac

200ml (7fl oz) beef stock

1 bay leaf

250ml (9fl oz) crème fraîche

Green beans with Parma ham

230g (8¼oz) green beans, trimmed

4 slices of Parma ham

1 tbsp butter

Preheat the oven to 220°C (425°F), Gas Mark 7. Put a little oil in a sauté pan, add the shallots and fry until they begin to go soft and translucent. Remove them from the pan and set aside.

Season the fillet with salt and pepper. Heat more oil and the butter in the sauté pan over a medium heat. Add the meat and leave it to sear for a couple of minutes until browned. Do this on all sides then remove from the pan. Spread the cracked pepper out on a plate. Smear the beef with mustard and roll in the cracked pepper, then place on a wire rack set over a roasting tin. The benefit of this is that the meat cooks more evenly because it is not sitting directly on the tin, which gets much hotter. Bake in the oven for about 35 minutes, then switch off the oven, open the door and leave the beef to rest for 10–15 minutes.

To make the sauce, put the reserved shallots and Cognac in a medium saucepan over a high heat. Boil for a couple of minutes then add the stock and bay leaf. Leave to boil merrily away until reduced by half.

Meanwhile, bring a pan of salted water to the boil, add the beans and boil for about 4 minutes, then drain. Divide the beans into 4 piles. Take one pile and wrap Parma ham tightly around it. Repeat with the other 3 piles. Season with salt (not too much as the Parma ham is salty) and some pepper. Heat the butter in a frying pan over a medium heat, add the beans and fry gently for a minute or two until the ham is crisp.

When the sauce has reduced, add the sautéed shallots and cook for 1 minute. Gradually add the crème fraîche, stirring all the time, then cook until the sauce is heated through. Place the beef fillet on a warmed serving plate. Pour the sauce over the meat and serve with the green beans wrapped in Parma ham.

Pork with Calvados,
caramelised apples & mustard mash

Pork, Calvados, mustard? A marriage made in heaven. Serves 4

1 4-bone 1.2kg (2½lb) piece of pork, cleaned

60g (2½oz) butter

8 Granny Smith apples: 4 peeled, cored and roughly chopped, reserving the peel and 4 cored and quartered

2 tbsp light brown sugar

3 sprigs rosemary

Juice of ½ lemon

1–2 tbsp vegetable oil

Salt and freshly ground black pepper

3 large onions, peeled and roughly chopped

1 sprig thyme

250ml (9fl oz) Calvados or dry cider

300ml (11fl oz) chicken stock

Scrape the pork bones clean, tie the meat up with string and leave to come to room temperature so that it cooks more evenly.

Preheat the oven to 180°C (350°F), Gas Mark 4.

To make the apple sauce, melt 20g (¾oz) of the butter in a pan and add the peeled and roughly chopped apples. Add 1 tablespoon of the sugar and 1 sprig of rosemary. Put a lid on the pan and cook for 5–10 minutes over a low heat. Then squeeze in the lemon juice, turn up the heat and boil it until the mixture thickens. Whizz this mixture up in a blender, then squash it through a sieve and set aside to cool.

Heat 1–2 tablespoons of oil in a large sauté pan with an ovenproof handle or a casserole dish. Season the pork with salt and pepper. Sear the meat on all sides and cook the fatty side for longer over a low heat to render down the fat. Add the onions to the pan with 1 sprig of rosemary and the thyme. The pork will begin to go nice and crispy. Once this happens, pop the pan into the oven for 40–45 minutes. After 20 minutes, give the mixture around the pork a stir.

Whilst this is cooking, make the caramelised apples. Melt the rest of the butter in a small pan and add the quartered apples, the remaining sprig of rosemary and the remaining sugar. Cook gently until the apples begin to caramelise and go soft. Set aside and keep warm.

Once the pork is done, remove it from the oven and put it on a plate to 'rest'. Put the Calvados or dry cider in the pan which contained the pork and boil it like mad until the mixture has reduced by half. Add the

▶

chicken stock and reduce by half again. If this mixture is looking a little lumpy, place a sieve over a jug and pour the sauce into it, leaving behind any lumps. The sauce may look a little thin – if so just add 1 or 2 tablespoons of the apple sauce to give it more body

Heat the apple sauce through gently. Slice up the pork and serve with the caramelised apples, apple sauce, Calvados sauce and mustard mash.

Mustard mash

4 baking potatoes

80g (3oz) butter

Salt and freshly ground black pepper

A dollop of good wholegrain mustard

A little English mustard, to taste

Preheat the oven to 220°C (425°F), Gas Mark 7, unless it's already being used for the pork.

Prick the potatoes all over and wrap each one in foil. Bake for 1 hour, or until a knife inserted into the centre of the potato glides through easily with no resistance. If cooking the potatoes at the same time as the pork (in which case your oven will be busy, and too cool), boil the potatoes in their skins in a saucepan, until tender.

Remove the potatoes from the oven and slice in half, then scoop the fluffy goodness into a saucepan and add the butter. Mix well over a low heat, then season to taste with salt and pepper and add enough wholegrain mustard to give a good flavour. I supplement the wholegrain with a bit of English mustard to get some heat into the mash and fire in the belly.

Trout en Papillote
with Sauternes & almonds

A superfast dish, requiring minimal effort but punching high on the flavour chart. Serves 4

4 trout, gutted and washed

1 lemon, cut into 12 small wedges, plus finely grated zest of 2 lemons

1 small bulb of fennel, trimmed and finely sliced

Half a bunch of spring onions, white bit only, trimmed and finely sliced lengthways from top to bottom

1 clove of garlic, peeled and sliced

2 handfuls of flaked almonds, toasted (see page 44)

150ml (5fl oz) Sauternes or white wine

Few glugs of olive oil

Salt and freshly ground black pepper

Preheat the oven to 200°C (400°F), Gas Mark 6.

Cut out 4 large circles of baking paper, each big enough to encase a fish. Arrange a trout in the centre of each paper, and using a really sharp knife, make 3 slashes across the fish. Put a small wedge of lemon in each slash, then divide the fennel, spring onions and garlic equally among the fish. Sprinkle some toasted flaked almonds over the top.

Add a couple of tablespoons of Sauternes and a couple of glugs of olive oil to the fish and season with salt and pepper. Wrap up each parcel so it is airtight, then place the parcels on a large baking tray and bake in the oven for 10–15 minutes, or until the flesh is firm. Serve 'en papillote' for guests to eat at the table.

Serve on the Thursday before payday (trout is über cheap) with some boiled potatoes and green beans.

Tomato & basil
Tarte Tatin

A bright and beautiful savoury tarte tatin which looks stunning on the plate. Serves 8 *(V)*

1 quantity of puff pastry
(see page 218) or 500g
(1lb 2oz) shop-bought puff
pastry

40 vine-ripened cherry
tomatoes

2 tbsp vegetable oil

Large pinch of sea salt

Freshly ground black
pepper

1 squidge of honey or
1 tbsp caster sugar

Handful of breadcrumbs

Plain flour, for dusting

1 egg, lightly beaten

Small bunch of fresh mint or
basil leaves

2 tbsp extra-virgin olive oil,
for drizzling

Equipment

20cm (8in) ovenproof frying
pan. If you don't have one,
cook the tomatoes in a
frying pan, then transfer to
a 20cm (8in) sandwich
cake tin for baking

Preheat the oven to 200°C (400°F), Gas Mark 6.

If making homemade pastry, make according to the recipe on page 218.

Place the tomatoes in the frying pan with the vegetable oil, salt and pepper
and honey or sugar. Arrange together as tightly as possible. Sprinkle the
tomatoes with the breadcrumbs – this will soak up some of the juice which
comes out of the tomatoes during cooking. On a well-floured work surface,
roll out a circle of puff pastry the same size as the top of the frying pan.
Place the puff pastry over the tomatoes, tucking it around them so the
tomatoes are encased.

Brush the pastry with the lightly beaten egg on the top only. It does seem
a bit pointless as this will be the underneath of the tart, but I like that bit
of extra crunch that it adds to the pastry and it looks so much more
presentable for that minute before you turn it upside down!

Bake in the oven for 20 minutes, or until the puff pastry is well puffed
and golden brown. Remove from the oven and leave to sit for a few
minutes, then tip away the excess liquid (if any) and put a large plate
upside down on top of the frying pan. Using oven gloves, press the plate
down hard and then quickly flip the whole thing so the frying pan is
upside down and the plate is on the bottom. I do this over the sink
because there is usually some leakage!

Remove the frying pan. Once the tart is cold, rip up some mint or basil
leaves and drizzle with extra-virgin olive oil. Add salt and pepper if
required. Serve cold with cold meats, cheeses, olives or salads.

Blueberry & lemon
Millefeuille

A simple and elegant dinner-party dessert. Serves 6 *(V)*

115g (4oz) icing sugar, plus extra for dusting

250g (9oz) shop-bought puff pastry

200g (7oz or 1 punnet) blueberries

Cream

165g (5½oz) whipping cream

25g (1oz) icing sugar

Seeds of 1 vanilla pod or 2 drops of vanilla extract

Finely grated zest of 1 lemon and a squeeze of juice

Hot chocolate sauce

165ml (5½fl oz) double cream

100g (3½oz) good milk or dark chocolate (or a combo of both), finely chopped or grated

25g (1oz) butter

1 generous tbsp golden syrup

Equipment

Piping bag fitted with a 1cm (½in) straight nozzle

Line a large baking tray with baking paper. Dust the work surface with lots of icing sugar and roll out the pastry to a rectangle just larger than 27 x 30cm (10½ x 12in), trimming the edges straight. It should be super thin, as thin as you can get it. Cut out 18 rectangles about 9cm (3½in) long and 5cm (2in) wide and place them on the prepared baking tray. Sprinkle with lots of icing sugar and put in the fridge for 30 minutes.

Preheat the oven to 200°C (400°F), Gas Mark 6.

Remove the pastry from the fridge and bake in the oven for 5 minutes, then remove from the oven and sprinkle the pastry with more icing sugar. Return to the oven and bake for a further 5 minutes, or until the pastry turns a golden brown. Remove from the oven and set aside.

For the cream, put the cream, icing sugar and vanilla in a large bowl and whip until medium-stiff peaks form. Fold in the lemon zest and juice to taste, then scoop the mixture into a piping bag fitted with a 1cm (½in) straight nozzle.

To make the chocolate sauce, heat the cream in a pan until just boiling. Remove the pan from the heat, add the chocolate and butter, don't stir and leave to stand for 5 minutes, then stir until everything is just mixed in and looks smooth and uniform. Add the golden syrup and stir a couple of times. Set aside.

Place one of the pastry thins on a serving plate. Pipe blobs of cream over the pastry (see picture) and put the blueberries between the cream then put another pastry thin on top and repeat with one more layer. Sprinkle the top layer with more icing sugar and repeat until all the pastries and cream are used up. Serve with the hot chocolate sauce poured all over.

Mango & passion fruit
Charlotte Russe

A Charlotte Russe is a firm-set mousse lined with sponge fingers. The mousse is made in dariole moulds, but there's no need to go splashing out on lots of new equipment – you can just use a ramekin instead, or a regular-sized coffee mug lined with cling film and half-filled with the mixture. Serves 4

Vegetable oil or oil spray, for oiling

4 leaves of gelatine (check on the packet how much is needed to set 570–600ml/1 pint liquid)

2 large perfectly ripe mangoes, pulp only, plus 1 mango, finely diced

4 passion fruit, juice only (reserve seeds for decoration)

40g (1½oz) icing sugar, plus extra to serve

450ml (16fl oz) double cream, plus about 100ml (4fl oz) double cream for assembly

1 bunch of fresh mint, ripped

Sponge fingers (or use shop-bought)

3 eggs

Seeds of ½ vanilla pod

180g (6½oz) caster sugar, plus extra for sprinkling

150g (5oz) plain flour

Oil the dariole moulds and line them with clingfilm, making sure it is hanging over the edges. This makes it easy to take the mousse out once it is set.

Put the gelatine in a bowl, completely cover with cold water and set aside.

Whiz the mangoes in a blender to a pulp then stir in the passion fruit juice. Put a sieve over a small pan and pour the pulp into the sieve. Squash as much as the mixture through with a wooden spoon, then add the sugar and stir over a low heat. Discard the pulp left in the sieve.

Heat until the sugar has dissolved and then remove the pan from the heat. Leave to stand for 2 minutes.

Take the gelatine leaves from the water – they should be floppy now – and squeeze out all the water, then put them in the hot mango and passion fruit liquid. Leave for 10 seconds then stir well until all the gelatine has dissolved and there are no lumps. Set the fruit mix aside.

Put the 450ml (16fl oz) cream in a large bowl and whip until it begins to thicken. Pour the mango mixture into the cream and fold together gently with a metal spoon. Pour this into a jug (it makes it easier to handle) and divide the mixture among the dariole moulds. Level the tops with the back of a small spoon and fold the excess clingfilm draped over the sides lightly over the top of the mousse. Put in the fridge for 1–1½ hours to set.

Mango & passion fruit
Charlotte Russe *(cont.)*

Equipment

4 dariole moulds

Piping bag fitted with a large straight piping nozzle

2m (6½ft) ribbon (optional)

While the mousse is setting, make the sponge fingers – if you are not using ready-made ones. Preheat the oven to 180°C (350°F), Gas Mark 4. Oil and line a large baking tray with baking paper.

Whisk the eggs and vanilla together in a large bowl until they begin to thicken then add the sugar in a steady stream stirring all the time. This will take about 10 minutes with an electric mixer but by hand it will take a lot longer.

Add the flour and, using as few stirs as possible, mix the flour in slowly with a metal spoon.

Put the mixture into a piping bag fitted with a large straight piping nozzle and pipe about 30–34 sponge fingers onto the prepared baking tray, spaced about 3cm (1¼in) apart. They need to be just longer than the height of the dariole mould. Sprinkle them with some caster sugar and bake in the oven for 5–7 minutes, or until they are spongy to the touch. You might need to bake these in a couple of batches. Remove from the oven and set aside.

Once the mousses feel firm to the touch, turn them upside down onto individual serving plates. Lift off the moulds and then peel off the clingfilm.

Stick the sponge fingers around the mousse vertically, close together so

there are no gaps. They need to be straight and upright like a sponge finger picket fence. It can be a fiddly job initially and if the sponge fingers are stubbornly refusing to stay stuck to the side of the mousse, whip up the remaining cream, dab a hazelnut-sized amount on the flat side of the finger and use it like glue to stick the fingers on. Be careful not to put too much cream on otherwise it will squeeze through the gaps and look unsightly. There may be some sponge fingers left over, these can be frozen or served dipped into melted chocolate and some chopped nuts.

Although my cookery lecturer would not approve (she always said, never put anything on the plate which you cannot eat), the prettiest way to present these is by tying them gently with ribbon. Not only do these look almost too good to eat, but the ribbon has another purpose of holding the sponge fingers securely in place.

Put a small dollop on top of each mousse (again to act as edible glue) and then place the chopped mango on top. Finish with ripped up mint leaves.

Best served to difficult-to-please guests.

Mascarpone & ginger
Crème Brûlée

There is much ado regarding the humble beginnings of this baked custard dish. The French claim it is theirs, but food historians say its origins lie in the kitchens of Cambridge University's Trinity College. For the best results, this recipe should be started the day before, to allow the ginger to infuse with the cream. However, if you are in a real hurry, then steep for an hour and add a pinch of ground ginger to boost the flavour. Serves 4–6 (V)

450ml (16fl oz) whipping or double cream

100g (3½oz) mascarpone

Seeds of 1 vanilla pod or 2 tsp vanilla extract

10cm (4in) long, thumb-width piece of fresh ginger, peeled and very finely grated

6 egg yolks

60g (2½oz) soft light brown sugar, plus about 4–6 tbsp for the topping

Equipment

4 ramekins (about 250ml/9fl oz capacity) or 6 shallow dishes

Preheat the oven to 150°C (300°F), Gas Mark 2. Put the ramekins in a roasting tin along with enough hot water to come halfway up their sides. Put the cream, mascarpone and vanilla in a pan and heat until almost boiling, then remove the pan from the heat and add the ginger.

In a small bowl, whisk the egg yolks and sugar together until they are pale and fluffy. Gradually add the ginger cream, whisking all the time. I like to include the bits of ginger in the crème brûlée, but if you don't want them, place a sieve over a measuring jug and pour the cream mix into it to sieve out the ginger. Using a wooden spoon, push the ginger mix left in the sieve to get as much flavour as you can, then discard the ginger bits.

Pour the cream mix equally into the shallow dishes, then place them (still in the roasting tin) in the oven for about 30 minutes, (if you have used ramekins they may take slightly longer) or until the brûlées begin to set. They should still wobble like jelly in the very centre but should not be too liquid, nor completely set. It is very easy to overcook these so check after 20 minutes to see how they are doing. Then check every 5 minutes after that, as some ovens are much more powerful than others.

Remove the brûlées from the oven and from the roasting tin and leave to cool right down, then place in the fridge for at least 1 hour. This is a brilliant dish for entertaining as you can make them to this stage, then keep in the fridge and finish them just before you're ready to serve.

Sprinkle about 1 tablespoon of brown sugar evenly on the top of each brûlée, making sure the tops are completely covered. Using a cook's blowtorch, caramelise the sugar until dark brown and crisp. A very hot grill works okay too, but a blowtorch is more fun. Leave to cool a little and then serve immediately.

Mini
Tiramisu

The nobility of posh dinner-party puds, but with the playfulness of a cupcake. Makes 12 (V)

165g (5½oz) soft butter

100g (3½oz) light brown sugar

100g (3½oz) caster sugar

4 eggs

260g (9oz) self-raising flour

80g (3oz) ricotta cheese

3 tbsp coffee essence
or 2 tbsp coffee dissolved
in 4 tbsp water

12 amaretti biscuits,
roughly crumbled

Icing sugar and cocoa
powder, for dusting

Filling

500g (1lb 2 oz) mascarpone

Seeds of 1 vanilla pod or
2 drops of vanilla extract

4 tbsp icing sugar

4 tbsp Marsala

8 amaretti biscuits, roughly
crumbled

Sugar syrup

165g (5½oz) granulated
sugar

165ml (5½fl oz) water

2 tbsp coffee essence or
2 tbsp coffee powder

Equipment

12-hole muffin tin

Preheat the oven to 180°C (350°F), Gas Mark 4. Line a muffin tin with 12 muffin cases.

Put the butter and sugars in a large bowl and cream together until light and fluffy. Add half the eggs, then tip in half the flour and stir well. Repeat with the rest of the egg then sift in the remaining flour. Add the ricotta, coffee and biscuits and mix well.

Using an ice-cream scoop or two dessertspoons, divide the mixture among the muffin cases. Spread the mixture flat with the back of a spoon. Bake in the oven for 25–30 minutes, or until a skewer inserted into the centre of the cupcake comes out clean. Remove from the oven and leave to cool.

The filling and syrup can be made while the cakes are baking. Mix together all the filling ingredients and set aside in the fridge.

Put all the syrup ingredients in a pan over a low heat and let the sugar dissolve. Turn up the heat and boil for a couple of minutes or until thick, then remove the pan from the heat and leave to cool.

Once the cakes are cooked, remove from the oven and leave to cool in the tin. Once you can handle them, remove each cake from the case and slice in half horizontally. Put the halves cut-side up on a large plate. Brush each liberally with the sugar syrup. Go mad here, the cakes should be really, really moist. Keep the rest of the syrup to pour over the cakes at the table.

Sandwich the halves back together with a generous dollop of the mascarpone cream, dust the tops with icing sugar and cocoa powder and serve straightaway.

Baked Alaskas
with orange liqueur & strawberries

I recently read about someone in America who had invented a counter-dessert to the baked Alaska – they'd called it a 'Frozen Florida'. I'm not sure it'll catch on …
Serves 4 *(V)*

180g (6oz) strawberries, hulled

1 tsp orange liqueur or orange juice

Twist of black pepper

1 tbsp caster sugar

4 round scoops of vanilla ice cream

1 ready-made Madeira sponge cake

Icing sugar, for dredging

Meringue

115g (4oz) caster sugar

2 pasteurised egg whites (available from the supermarket in a carton in the fridge section)

Blitz about two-thirds of the strawberries with the orange liqueur, black pepper and caster sugar in a blender or food processor. Transfer the mixture to a bowl. Slice the remaining strawberries and add to the bowl. Put in the fridge for at least 30 minutes.

Preheat the oven to 250°C (500°F), Gas mark 10. Line a small baking tray with baking paper.

Use an ice-cream scoop to dollop 4 large balls of ice cream onto the lined baking tray and place in the fridge.

Cut out 4 circles of sponge cake, the same diameter as the ice cream balls, and place on a large baking tray. Brush the cake pieces with some of the strawberry purée. Divide the sliced strawberries between the cake pieces, then put the ice-cream balls on top of the strawberries. You may need to squash them down a bit to make them stick, as the ice cream slips and slides around. Put in the freezer to harden.

To make the meringue, put the caster sugar in a bowl with 1 egg white and whisk with an electric whisk until the mixture starts to go opaque, shiny and thick. Add the remaining egg white and whisk well until the

▶

mixture forms a stiff peak. If the mixture looks runny, keep on whisking; it will stiffen eventually! This is not the usual way of making a meringue but it's great as it works every time and the whites are not overwhisked. The resulting meringue is super, super shiny, stiff and stable.

Take one of the ice-cream sponge balls from the freezer and dollop the meringue all over it, taking it right down the sides to cover the sponge and ice cream completely. Use a wide knife or a palette knife to make spikes stick out all over the meringue. Put it on the baking tray (the one you will use to cook it on) and place back in the freezer. Repeat with the rest of the ice-cream balls. It is important that the ice cream is really hard before the Alaskas go in the oven.

Once you have covered all of them, remove the tray from the freezer and dredge the Alaskas lightly with icing sugar. Bake in the oven until the meringue begins to colour. Keep watching it the whole time as this should only take a couple of minutes. I have taken it too far and burnt it at this stage too many times! Alternatively, you can use a cook's blowtorch to brown the Alaskas. Now remove from the oven and serve immediately, accompanied by any remaining strawberry purée, if you like.

Passion & lime
Meringue Pie

When you need a recipe that is easy to prepare and doesn't require too many ingredients, this is the one. More impressive than the ubiquitous Eton Mess or strawberry meringue, but just as refreshing and fruity, this dessert is perfect for a summer tea party on the lawn, or anywhere. This pie also transports really well, so you can bake it at home and then take it to all those special occasions with friends and family.

Serves 6–8 (V)

1 quantity of shortcrust pastry (see page 220) or 375g (13oz) shop-bought sweet shortcrust pastry

Plain flour, for dusting

Passion fruit filling

12 small passion fruit

6 tbsp cornflour

150ml (5fl oz) water

360g (12oz) caster sugar

Juice and finely grated zest of 4 limes

5 egg yolks

Meringue

230g (8½oz) caster sugar

4 egg whites

Tiny squeeze of lemon juice

Equipment

20cm (8in) loose-bottomed tart tin

Preheat the oven to 180°C (350°F), Gas Mark 4.

Roll out the pastry on a well-floured work surface to the thickness of just less than a £1 coin. Line the tart tin with the pastry, then put in the fridge for about 30 minutes, or until firm.

Once the pastry is firm, remove it from the fridge and trim the edges (see page 120). Take a piece of baking paper slightly larger than the tart and scrunch it up, then unscrunch it and line the tart with it. Fill it with baking beans or dried beans and 'blind bake' in the oven for 20–25 minutes, or until the pastry is a light golden brown and feels sandy to the touch. Remove the baking beans and paper and cook for a further 5 minutes to dry out the bottom of the pastry, if necessary. Once cooked, remove the pastry case from the oven and set aside. Turn the oven down to 150°C (300°F), Gas Mark 2.

To make the filling, put the pulp and juice of the passion fruit in a sieve set over a bowl, then using a wooden spoon, press the mixture through the sieve. This takes a bit of time but it is the best way to make sure all the juice and pulp are extracted, leaving the pips behind. Take half the seeds left in the sieve and add them to the passion fruit juice. It is best not to have all the seeds otherwise it would be too crunchy.

Put the cornflour in a small pan and, while stirring, gradually add the water. Add the sugar, passion fruit pulp and lime zest and juice and heat gently until the mixture boils and thickens. Remove the pan from the heat and leave to cool for a few minutes. Stir in the egg yolks, then set aside and keep warm.

▶

Passion & lime meringue pie *(cont.)*

For the meringue, put all the sugar in a bowl with 1 of the egg whites and a tiny squeeze of lemon juice. Using an electric hand whisk, whisk for 1 minute. Add 2 more egg whites and keep whisking until the mixture becomes very stiff and shiny. Add the last egg white and whisk again until the mixture becomes stiff and shiny. This is a backward way of doing a meringue but it is impossible to overwhisk it and you will have the stiffest shiniest meringue you can imagine. If the eggs are added too quickly the mixture will look quite runny, but keep whisking and it will go stiff, although it can take some time.

Pour the warm filling mixture into the tart case, then dollop the meringue over the top. Use a fork to make spikes all over the meringue then bake in the oven for 20–30 minutes, or until the meringue is crisp.

Remove from the oven and leave to cool completely.

Super speedy
Chocolate Mousse

Easy, tasty chocolate mousse. Puddings made simple. Serves 4

400ml (14fl oz) whipping or double cream

Seeds of 1 vanilla pod or 2 drops of vanilla extract

140g (5oz) dark chocolate, melted (see page 45)

140g (5oz) milk chocolate, melted (see page 45)

40g (1½oz) dark chocolate, to decorate

Equipment

4 Martini glasses or 4 ramekins

Whip the cream and vanilla together in a large bowl until it just begins to thicken. Pour in the melted chocolates and slowly stir everything together with a whisk until the mixture is smooth, then whisk for 2–3 minutes until it has thickened. Spoon the mixture into the glasses and put in the fridge for at least 30 minutes to set.

Remove the mousse from the fridge, grate over the chocolate to decorate and serve.

Brandy Snaps

These are truly retro but always create lots of smiles when brought out at a special occasion. Make them big enough to serve on their own or small enough to use as a garnish for a plated dessert. You could also shape them into 'cups', over the end of an oiled rolling pin, then fill with cream and fresh fruit for something a bit different.
Makes 15 brandy snaps (V)

Vegetable oil, for oiling

50g (2oz) butter

50g (2oz) soft light brown sugar

50g (2oz) golden syrup

50g (2oz) plain flour

Pinch of ground cinnamon

Pinch of ground ginger

Pinch of finely grated lemon zest

Filling

150ml (11fl oz) double cream

1 tbsp icing sugar

2 tsp Armagnac

Equipment

Piping bag

Preheat the oven to 180°C (350°F), Gas Mark 4. Line two baking sheets with baking paper.

Put the butter, sugar and golden syrup in a medium pan and stir over a low heat until melted. Remove the pan from the heat and add the flour, cinnamon, ginger and lemon zest. Beat until smooth and leave to stand for about 30 minutes, until the mixture firms up.

Cooking the brandy snaps should be done in small batches, as they must be shaped the minute they come out of the oven. Put 4–6 rounded teaspoonfuls of the mixture on each lined baking sheet, spacing them about 10cm (4in) apart. Bake this first batch in the oven for about 8 minutes, until the edges begin to darken a little; keep an eye on them as they burn easily. Remove from the oven and leave to stand for 2–3 minutes, until they firm up slightly but are still very pliable. Using a lightly oiled palette knife, lift one from the tray and wrap it loosely around the oiled handle of a wooden spoon in the classic brandy snap shape (see photo). Hold it in place for a minute until it hardens, then slip it off the handle and set aside. Repeat with the remaining brandy snaps on the tray. Cook and shape the rest of the mixture in the same way.

To make the filling, put the cream and icing sugar in a bowl and whip until medium-stiff peaks form, then fold in the Armagnac. Fill a piping bag with the cream and pipe into the brandy snap tubes for full dramatic effect!

Sweet Treats

I am thrilled to have a chapter dedicated to sweet treats. It's full of those naughty little 'snackettes' that we really shouldn't be eating, but which are just so hard to say no to. Sometimes, when your day has been less than satisfactory, the best solution is to make a plateful of one of these fine fancies and to nibble pleasurably without a hint of guilt. And once you've sampled my Cookies and Cream Fudge Brownies, you'll wonder how on earth you survived this long without them!

'There is nothing better than a friend, unless it is a friend with chocolate.'

Charles Dickens
Novelist
1812 – 1870

Fondant Fancies

This recipe is more involved than others, but it's worth pushing the baking boat out now and again for an exceedingly accomplished result. Makes about 16 *(V)*

165g (5½oz) butter, softened

165g (5½oz) caster sugar, plus extra for sprinkling

3 eggs

165g (5½oz) self-raising flour

Pinch of salt

Buttercream

200g (7oz) butter, softened

400g (14oz) icing sugar

Seeds of 1 vanilla pod or 2 drops of vanilla extract

Filling and topping

200g (7oz) natural marzipan

Icing sugar, for dusting

80g (3oz), apricot jam, plus 2 tbsp water, warmed and cooled (see page 53)

200g (7oz) fondant icing

100g (3½oz) Royal icing

Food colouring (optional)

100g (3½oz) milk or dark chocolate, melted (see page 45), optional

Preheat the oven to 180°C (350°F), Gas Mark 4 and put the middle shelf in position. Line the baking tin with baking paper.

Put the butter and sugar in a large bowl and cream together until pale and fluffy. Add one egg and half the flour and beat well. Add the remaining eggs and the flour and beat well again.

Dollop the mixture into the prepared tin and level with a palette knife. Bake in the oven for 30 minutes, or until a skewer inserted in the thickest part comes out clean. Remove from the oven and flip upside down onto a wire rack. Lift out of the tin and leave to cool on the wire rack.

Meanwhile, prepare the marzipan. Roll out the marzipan on a well-sugared board to around half a £1 coin thickness. Roll it out to slightly larger than the size of the sponge. Once the cake is cool, peel off the baking paper that it was baked in. This top side should now be nice and flat. Spread the apricot jam over this side and then carefully lay the marzipan over the sponge. This is quite tricky and the marzipan can tear but it is very easy to patch it up. Trim off any excess with scissors. Place the sponge in the fridge for about 30 minutes, or until firm.

Meanwhile, make the buttercream. Put the butter, icing sugar and vanilla in a bowl and whisk until it becomes pale and fluffy.

Remove the sponge from the fridge and slice in half horizontally. Spread with the buttercream and sandwich back together. Pop back in the fridge while you prepare the fondant icing.

▼

▶

Fondant fancies *(cont.)*

Equipment

20cm (8in) square baking tin

Small piping bag fitted with a tiny round nozzle

For the fondant icing, make the icing almost to the packet instructions, they tend to say to add too much water on the packet and you want this icing to be thick enough not to drop off the cake once it has been put on. If you're using food colouring, divide the icing among three bowls and colour each one with the colouring of your choice.

Remove the cake from the fridge and cut it into 16 equal squares. Have a wire rack ready with baking paper underneath it to catch all the drips. Take a piece of the sponge on a fork and hold the top lightly with your forefinger. This is messy work and very time consuming but the results really do speak for themselves, so it is well worth the perseverance.

Dip the sponge square into the coloured icing of your choice – dip it right down until the whole thing is covered then place on the wire rack to set. Repeat with all the squares. If, as does so often happen, you find your fondant icing is riddled with sponge bits, simply strain the fondant icing to remove them.

While this icing is setting make your Royal icing according to the packet instructions. Again, you can colour this if you want to with the food colouring. Fill a small piping bag fitted with a tiny round nozzle with the icing and pipe decorations on top of the iced cakes. If you don't want to go to the bother of using Royal icing you can just melt some chocolate and flick it over the top. Leave to harden.

These little cakes keep for up to three days in an airtight container. Serve with tea and biscuits.

Dreamlike
Shortbread

Also known as 'my Grandma's shortbread', this is a rare family recipe passed down from my Polish grandmother. Lovely for a Christmas or birthday treat, or for an indulgent Saturday afternoon, with tea and an old movie. Makes 8 dainty pieces *(V)*

130g (4½oz) butter, softened

60g (2½oz) caster sugar, plus extra for sprinkling

130g (4½oz) plain flour

60g (2½oz) rice flour

Pinch of salt

Equipment

20cm (8in) loose-bottomed sandwich cake tin

Put the butter and sugar in a large bowl and cream together until pale and fluffy. Add the plain flour, rice flour and salt, and stir well until the mixture is smooth and uniform. I find it easiest to keep pressing the mixture against the side of the bowl to mix it. Bring the mixture together and press into the tin, smoothing it with the back of a spoon. Crimp the edges by pressing with the tips of two fingers, or two knuckles, then mark into 8 pieces with a knife and prick each triangle three times with a fork. Put in the fridge for 30 minutes to firm up. Preheat the oven to 170°C (325°F), Gas Mark 3.

Remove the shortbread from the fridge and bake in the oven for 30–35 minutes, or until it is a very light golden colour. Remove the shortbread from the oven and sprinkle over some caster sugar. Leave to cool in the tin for a few minutes before removing it from the tin and cooling on a wire rack. Once cold, cut into 8 pieces and serve.

Variation Add a tablespoon of grated stem ginger or the finely grated zest of 1 lemon or lime.

Bite-size
Jam Doughnuts

Making your own doughnuts at home is so much fun! Definite party food, and children simply love them. *Makes about 40 doughnuts (V)*

Dough

210ml (1½fl oz) milk

15g (½oz) unsalted butter

1 egg

150g (5oz) strong white bread flour, plus extra for dusting

200g (7oz) plain flour

1 x 7g sachet fast-action dried yeast

2 tbsp soft light brown sugar

¼ tsp salt

1 tsp ground cinnamon (optional)

Squeeze of lemon juice

1 litre (1¾ pints) vegetable oil, for deep-frying, plus extra for oiling

150g (5oz) warmed raspberry jam or 150ml (5fl oz) creme patissière (see page 225)

▼

Put the milk in a saucepan and heat gently until warm, then add the butter and continue to heat until it has melted. Remove the pan from the heat and beat in the egg.

Put the flours, yeast, sugar, salt and cinnamon, if using, in a bowl and stir together well. Make a hole in the centre of the mixture and pour in the milk mixture and the lemon juice to make a soft but not sticky dough. Knead the dough on a floured surface for 10 minutes by hand or for 5 minutes in an electric mixer fitted with a dough hook.

Once the dough is well kneaded, pull off a small piece the size of a 2-p coin, roll into a ball and place on a lined baking tray. Repeat with the rest of the dough until you have about 40 balls. Space them about 3cm (1¼in) apart to give them room to rise. Cover the tray loosely with oiled clingfilm, making sure it is airtight. Leave in a warm place for 45 minutes, or until they have increased in size.

Once the dough is nicely risen, put the sugar and cinnamon, if using, for coating in a large bowl.

▶

Coating

100g (3½oz) caster sugar, plus extra for sprinkling

1 tbsp ground cinnamon (optional)

Equipment

Piping bag fitted with a nozzle

Heat the oil for deep-frying in a medium, deep pan. The oil should be hot enough that a small piece of bread will cook in 50 seconds. It can take 5 minutes or more for the oil to reach the right temperature. Once the oil is hot enough, remove the clingfilm from the doughnuts and lower two or three at a time into the hot oil, adding more until there are ten in the pan. Deep-fry them for 50 seconds, then using a slotted spoon, remove them from the oil, drain briefly on kitchen paper and toss them in the coating mixture and leave to cool. Repeat with the rest of the doughnuts. I usually turn off the heat once the oil is ready, as it normally retains its heat long enough to fry all of the doughnuts. If the doughnuts are taking too long to cook, just turn the heat back on for a minute or two, to bring it back to the right temperature.

Spoon the jam or crème patissière into the piping bag, laying the tip end down as you do this so the jam doesn't go shooting out of the bottom. Stick the nozzle into one of the doughnuts and fill it with as much jam as you like. Repeat with the rest of the doughnuts, then sprinkle with some more sugar and serve.

Macaroons

Beautiful macaroons are one of the current 'sweet' crazes. Make a batch, put them in a pretty box tied up with ribbon, and give them to a friend as a dazzling gift. Makes about 24 macaroons (12 if sandwiched together) (V)

125g (4½oz) icing sugar

125g (4½oz) ground almonds

40g (1½oz) egg whites

2 tbsp water

110g (4oz) caster sugar

50g (2oz) egg whites

Food colouring (optional)

Desiccated coconut, for sprinkling (optional)

150ml (5fl oz) double or whipped cream, whipped

Equipment

Piping bag fitted with a 1cm (½in) nozzle

Preheat the oven to 170°C (325°F), Gas Mark 5. Line a large baking tray with baking paper.

Put the icing sugar, ground almonds and egg whites together in a large bowl and mix to a paste.

Put the water and caster sugar in a small pan and heat gently to melt the sugar then turn up the heat and boil it until the mixture starts to go syrupy and thickens. I don't use a thermometer but it would read 115°C (239°F).

Whisk the egg whites in a small bowl until medium-stiff peaks form, then pour in the sugar syrup, whisking until the mixture becomes stiff and shiny. For coloured macaroons, add a few drops of food colouring. Tip this meringue mixture into the almond paste mixture and stir gently until the becomes stiff and shiny again.

Spoon into the piping bag. Pipe a little mixture under each corner of the baking paper to stop it sliding around. With the bag held vertically, pipe 4cm (1½in) flat circles onto the lined tray, about 2cm (¾in) apart, twisting the bag after each one. The mixture should be quite loose to give a smooth finish. The piping will leave a small 'tip' on each circle so, when they're all piped, give the tray 2–3 slams on a flat surface to flatten them. At this stage, sprinkle with desiccated coconut if you want. Leave to stand for 30 minutes to form a skin then bake in the oven for 12–15 minutes with the door slightly ajar, until firm. Remove from the oven, lift the paper off the baking tray and leave the macaroons to cool on the paper.

When cool, sandwich the macaroons together with whipped cream. They can be kept for a couple of days, if they hang around that long.

Irresistible peanut butter
Cookies

For the best-textured cookies, the trick is to stir in the peanut butter as little as possible. To satisfy my peanut fetish I like to sprinkle a handful of slightly toasted peanuts on top. Makes 12 (V)

130g (4½oz) butter, softened

200g (7oz) soft light brown sugar

1 egg

Seeds of 1 vanilla pod or 2 drops of vanilla extract

200g (7oz) plain flour

½ tsp baking powder

½ tsp bicarbonate of soda

300g (10½oz) peanut butter

Handful of lightly toasted peanuts (see page 44), optional

Preheat the oven to 170°C (325°F), Gas Mark 3.

Put the butter and sugar in a large bowl and cream together until pale and fluffy. Add the egg and vanilla and mix well, then stir in the flour, baking powder and bicarbonate of soda. Gently stir in the peanut butter then squidge the dough into a ball.

Divide the dough into 12 equal pieces and, using your hands, roll each one into a ball. Place on a large baking tray, spaced at least 10cm (4in) apart.

Flatten each one slightly with a fork, sprinkle over the peanuts, if using, and bake in the oven for 12–15 minutes, or until the cookies start to go golden brown. The cookies will still be soft when they come out of the oven but will firm up as they cool.

Remove from the oven and leave to cool on the baking tray.

Big yummy double
Choc Chip Cookies

Soft, chewy chocolate chip cookies. For a slightly healthier option, replace the cocoa powder with plain flour and the chocolate chips with nuts and raisins instead. *Makes 8 large American-style cookies (V)*

110g (4oz) butter, softened

200g(7oz) soft light brown sugar

1 egg

Seeds of 1 vanilla pod or 2 drops of vanilla extract

165g (5½oz) plain flour

Pinch of salt

½ tsp baking powder

½ tsp bicarbonate of soda

30g (1¼oz) cocoa powder

100g (3½oz) milk chocolate chips

100g (3½oz) dark chocolate chips

Preheat the oven to 190°C (375°F), Gas Mark 5. Line 2 large baking trays with baking paper.

Put the butter and sugar in a large bowl and cream together until combined. It does not need to be light and fluffy. I do this with my mixer but a hand whisk will do the job too. Stir in the egg and vanilla and mix well. It may look like it has curdled at this stage but not to worry. Give it a good whisk and it will come good. Add the flour, salt, baking powder, bicarbonate of soda and cocoa powder and mix until the dough looks uniform. The dough will be very stiff. Add the chocolate chips and mash everything in with a wooden spoon.

Divide the mixture into 9 balls and space about 10cm (4in) apart on the prepared baking tray. Bake in the oven for 10–12 minutes. The cookies will have a cracked top and will be very soft. Remove the cookies from the oven and leave to cool on the baking trays. They will quickly harden up as they cool.

Serve with the obligatory glass of ice-cold milk.

Flapjacks

There was a little girl, (okay, 5'10") who had a little curl (which she blow-dried straight daily) right in the middle of her forehead. When she was good, she was very, very good, and when she was bad, she made a batch of flapjacks and devoured the whole lot herself. Makes 12 *(V)*

175g (6oz) butter

175g (6oz) golden syrup

175g (6oz) muscovado sugar

350g (12oz) porridge oats

Finely grated zest of ½ lemon

Pinch of ground ginger

Equipment

20cm (8in) square baking tin

Preheat the oven to 150°C (300°F), Gas Mark 2. Line the baking tin with baking paper.

Melt the butter in a medium pan over a low heat. Dip a brush in the butter and brush the baking tin with a little bit of it. Add the golden syrup and sugar to the butter and heat gently. Once the sugar is dissolved and the butter is melted remove the pan from the heat and stir in the porridge oats, lemon zest and ginger.

Pack the mixture into the baking tin and squash down. Bake in the oven for 40 minutes.

Once cooked, remove from the oven, leave to cool for 15 minutes, then turn out on to a chopping board and cut into squares.

These flapjacks are delicious in a packed lunch or as a grab and go breakfast. To undo the healthiness of the oats, however, pour some melted dark chocolate over the cooked flapjacks and then leave to set before eating.

Cookies & cream
Fudge Brownies

When I was eight, chocolate brownies were my life. I scoured the local shops on my Raleigh bike, looking for gainful employment to support my chocolate brownie habit. The ironmonger's wife took pity on me and offered me a job paying £1 an hour to iron their smalls and sheets. After two hours I had enough cash to buy a couple of brownies, plus change for some sherbet lemons on the way home. It was worth every crease! *Makes 16 (V)*

165g (5½oz) butter, plus extra for greasing

200g (7oz) dark chocolate, grated or finely chopped

3 eggs

2 egg yolks

Seeds of 1 vanilla pod or 2 tsp vanilla extract

165g (5½oz) soft light brown sugar

2 tbsp plain flour

1 tbsp cocoa powder

Pinch of salt

154g pack of oreo biscuits, broken into quarters

Icing sugar, for dusting

Equipment

20cm (8in) square baking tin

Preheat the oven to 180°C (350°F), Gas Mark 6 with the middle shelf ready. Grease the baking tin, then line with baking paper with the paper overlapping the sides a little.

Melt the butter in a pan over a medium heat. When the butter has melted, remove the pan from the heat and add the grated chocolate. Leave to stand for a few minutes until the chocolate goes soft then stir together. Alternatively, you can put the chocolate and butter in bowl and melt in the microwave in 25-second blasts, stirring well each time.

Whisk the eggs, egg yolks and vanilla together in a large bowl until they begin to get light and fluffy. Add the sugar in two additions whisking between each. Pour it around the side of the egg mix so as not to knock out the air that has been whisked in to it. Keep whisking until the mixture becomes stiffer. Once the egg mixture is ready pour the chocolate into it, again around the sides so as not to knock the air out.

Add the flour, cocoa powder, salt and a third of the oreos and stir until fully combined, then pour the mixture into the prepared tin. Scatter the remaining oreos over the top, pressing them in slightly. Bake in the oven for 25–30 minutes. The middle should be very so slightly gooey.

Leave the brownies to cool in the tin. The top will sink and crack a little. Pull the brownies out using the overlapping paper and cut the brownies into squares. Dust with icing sugar.

Substitute oreos for toasted walnuts, pecans or sprinkle the brownies with honeycomb.

Baklava

Those on a diet, or with troublesome teeth, look away now. Moist, crunchy and gooey, Baklava are a sweet, sweet pastry, made from sugar, honey, nuts, butter and, well, more sugar. Splendid, especially after a lamb kebab with sugary mint tea. Makes 16 (V)

180g (6oz) butter, melted and cooled

2 x 270g (10oz) packets of filo pastry

150g (5oz) pecans and green pistachios, finely chopped, to decorate

Sugar syrup

340g (12oz) granulated sugar

200ml (7fl oz) water

3 tbsp honey

2 tsp orange-blossom water,

Finely grated zest of 1 lemon

Filling

200g (7oz) pecans, very finely chopped

300g (10½oz) green pistachios (or walnuts or almonds can be substituted), very finely chopped

2 tbsp soft light brown sugar

1 tsp mixed spice

Equipment

20cm (8in) square cake tin

To make the sugar syrup, put the granulated sugar, water and honey in a small pan over a low heat, stirring occasionally until the sugar dissolves. Add the orange-blossom water and lemon, bring the mixture to the boil, then reduce the heat and simmer gently for 5–10 minutes until the syrup thickens slightly. It should stick to the back of the spoon for just a second before sliding off and will look like watered-down honey. Remove the pan from the heat and leave to cool.

Preheat the oven to 180°C (350°F), Gas Mark 4. Mix all the filling ingredients together and set aside.

Use a silicone pastry brush (better than a natural one as the hairs don't shed!) to paint the tin with melted butter, then put 4–5 layers of filo pastry flat on the base, brushing each layer with melted butter. Depending on the size of your pastry, you may be able to fold each sheet in half to make 2 layers. If still bigger than the tin, fold in the edges. Sprinkle one-third of the filling evenly over the filo, and top with 4–5 more layers of buttered filo, folding neatly to fit. Add another third of the filling, then 4–5 more buttered filo layers, then the final filling third and the final 4–5 layers of buttery filo. Cut the baklava into 16 squares with a sharp knife.

Pour the remaining butter over the top layer of filo, so that all the pastry is covered in butter. Place the tin in the centre of the oven and cook for about 25–30 minutes, or until the pastry is golden brown and crisp.

Re-cut the baklava as soon as it comes out of the oven, then ladle the syrup over the top and sprinkle with the chopped nuts to decorate. Leave to cool before chilling in the fridge for 30 minutes, or until firm.

Use a spatula to ease out the first piece.

Honeycomb

My all-time favourite recipe to make: homemade honeycomb! Serves 8 *(V)*

Vegetable oil, for oiling
80g (3oz) butter
160g (5½oz) caster sugar
80g (3oz) golden syrup
2 tsp bicarbonate of soda

Equipment

20cm (8in) square baking
tin

Oil the baking tin.

Put the butter, sugar and golden syrup in a medium heavy-based pan and heat gently until the sugar has dissolved. Turn up the heat and boil rapidly, without stirring. If using a gas hob, make sure the flame doesn't 'lick' up the sides of the pan, as the sugar will start to burn on the sides of the pan. If some sugar does 'catch' at any point, dip a pastry brush in some water and brush the sides of the pan to remove any sugar. Keep an eye on it the whole time. If the mixture goes darker at one side of the mix, then gently swirl the pan to mix it all together. Keep boiling until the mixture goes a good golden 'honeycomb' colour – this will take about 5 minutes. Add the bicarbonate of soda and stir it for a few seconds. Tip the honeycomb into the oiled baking tin and leave until cold and set. Then cut or break into pieces to serve.

To give the kids a very naughty treat, dip the pieces in melted chocolate, or use small shards of honeycomb to stir into ice creams or decorate puddings. Or blitz to a dust and sprinkle over desserts.

Churros

This little number is a sinful treat from Spain or Latin America. The finished article has a magnificently crisp outer crust and a soft, tender interior. Dip in chocolate and serve with coffee for the perfect 4pm pick-me-up. *Makes 6–8 (V)*

60g (2½oz) butter

150ml (5fl oz) buttermilk or 150ml (5fl oz) milk plus a squeeze of lemon juice

70g (3oz) plain flour

Pinch of salt

1 tsp ground cinnamon

2–3 eggs

Vegetable oil for deep-frying

Hot chocolate sauce (see page 172), for dipping

Coating

100g (3½oz) caster sugar

1 tbsp ground cinnamon

Equipment

Piping bag fitted with a large star nozzle

Put the butter and buttermilk in a medium pan and set over a medium heat. Once the butter has melted, turn up the heat and bring to the boil, then immediately remove the pan from the heat and add the flour, salt and cinnamon. Stir vigorously until the mixture begins to come away from the sides of the pan, then set it aside to cool to body temperature.

Once cool, add the eggs one at a time, beating really hard after each addition. You will notice the mixture becomes shiny and glossy, this is just what you want. Place the mixture into a piping bag fitted with the biggest star piping nozzle you can find.

I always find deep-frying intimidating but as long as you have a lid nearby to cover the pan, never leave it unattended and don't let it get too hot, you should feel safe! At home I do my frying in a large heavy-based saucepan filled one-third with oil, as I don't own a deep-fryer. Heat the oil in a saucepan like this. The oil is ready when a small piece of bread browns in about 50 seconds. If it is too hot the churros will just burn and if too cool they won't crisp up.

Meanwhile, mix the sugar and cinnamon coating on a large plate.

Pipe a 15cm (6in) strip into the hot oil from a low height so the oil does not splash. Pipe three into the pan (no more or it may lower the temperature too much). Once they turn golden brown and begin to firm up they are done. This should take about 4 minutes, depending on the size of the churros and the oil temperature. Scoop them out using a slotted spoon and drain on kitchen paper. Immediately roll them in the cinnamon mixture and transfer to another plate. Repeat with all the mixture.

Serve with a hot chocolate sauce for dipping and a cup of hot cocoa.

Rosewater
Marshmallows

These marshmallows are piped into teardrop shapes rather than cut from a large block. It's a messy-to-make recipe and requires focus, focus, focus and lots of organisation. It may take a couple of times to get them right but, once you do, you'll want to make them again and again. Makes about 60 £2-coin-sized marshmallows

About 200g (7oz) icing sugar, for dusting

200g (7oz) cornflour, for dusting

12 sheets of gelatine

125ml (4½fl oz) water

50g (2oz) golden syrup

550g (1¼lb) granulated sugar

3 egg whites

Few drops of rosewater

Few drops of pink or red colouring

Equipment

1 large piping bag, fitted with a 1cm (½in) straight nozzle

Dust three large baking trays with icing sugar and cornflour. The trays should look like there has been a very heavy snowfall of icing sugar and cornflour and there should not be any 'tray' showing.

Fill a medium bowl with cold water and add the gelatine. Set aside.

Put the 125ml (4½fl oz) water, golden syrup and granulated sugar in a large pan over a medium heat and boil it for about 10 minutes. If done on a gas hob, use the largest ring on a medium flame. (Don't use a high flame or the sugary syrup will burn.) Keep boiling the mixture until it turns from a yellow to golden brown. The bubbles will go from being small and a bit frothy to a bit bigger (or 130°C/266°F on a sugar thermometer, if using, but it can be done without) and the syrup will coat the back of a spoon. If any bits of sugar start to go dark brown on the sides of the pan, dip a pastry brush in some water and brush the sides of the pan to remove them.

While this is boiling whisk the egg whites in a large bowl until medium-stiff peaks form, then set aside.

When the water, golden syrup and granulated sugar mixture is ready, turn off the heat. Remove the gelatine from the bowl of water and squeeze out the excess water, then carefully add it to the boiling sugar and syrup mix. It will foam up a little then calm down after a few seconds. Stir the mixture with the handle end of the wooden spoon to combine.

▶

Gradually add this mixture to the egg whites whisking all the time in a slow steady stream, taking care not to get the hot sugar syrup on the whisks. This whole process of whisking and pouring can be tricky so rope in a willing pair of hands if possible. Keep whisking this until super-stiff peaks form – it will look very glossy and very shiny and will be very, very stiff. Set aside. This may take 10–15 minutes with an electric mixer and allow a good 15–20 minutes with an electric hand whisk.

Once the marshmallows have reached this stage, stir in a few drops of rosewater and food colouring.

While the mixture is still warm, spoon it into a large piping bag fitted with a 1cm (½in) straight nozzle. Pipe blobs of the mixture onto the prepared baking tray, spaced about 2cm (¾in) apart. Continue until all of the mixture is used up, then dust with lots and lots of cornflour and icing sugar. Leave the marshmallows to set for an hour. If you find that after 1 hour the marshmallows are cool but not set (they will not be as firm as shop-bought ones, but they will hold their shape, be soft but not gooey in the centre), then leave them overnight covered in clingfilm and well doused in a mixture of cornflour and icing sugar. If in the morning they are still not set, alas, the marshmallows need to be made again.

Enjoy. Brilliant for a child's birthday party or as a great petit fours for a cool retro dinner party.

Whoopie Cakes

Will the Amish whoopie cake steal the crown from the mighty cupcake? The jury is most definitely out! The ingredients are similar – a combination of sponge cake and buttercream icing – but whoopie cakes present exciting new opportunities for creative decorating and artistic flair. You can have so much fun baking these and decorating them. These keep well in a sealed tin for a couple of days. *Makes about 10 (V)*

120ml (4½fl oz) milk

190g (6¾oz) demerara sugar

120ml (4½fl oz) soured cream

180g (6½oz) plain flour

½ tsp bicarbonate of soda

½ tsp baking powder

55g (2oz) cocoa powder

Pinch of salt

1 egg, plus 1 egg yolk

Seeds of 1 vanilla pod or 4 drops of vanilla extract

115ml (4¼fl oz) sunflower oil

Buttercream filling

200g (7oz) butter, softened

400g (14oz) icing sugar

Seeds of 1 vanilla pod or 4 drops of vanilla extract

1 tbsp milk

Equipment

Piping bag fitted with a large plain nozzle

Preheat the oven to 170°C (325°F), Gas Mark 3. Line 2 baking trays with baking paper.

Heat the milk gently in a small saucepan, add the sugar, then take the pan off the heat, add the soured cream and stir through to combine. Leave to cool to body temperature. Meanwhile, put the flour, bicarbonate of soda, baking powder, cocoa and salt together in a large bowl.

Once the milk mixture has cooled to body temperature, add the eggs, vanilla and oil to the pan and stir to just combine. Pour the liquid ingredients into the flour mixture and fold gently together.

Transfer the mixture into a piping bag fitted with a large nozzle and pipe circles about 8cm (3in) in diameter on to the lined baking trays, spaced about 8cm (3in) apart. Bake in the oven for 8–10 minutes, or until a skewer inserted in the thickest part comes out clean.

Leave the whoopie cakes to cool on the trays. Meanwhile, to make the buttercream, beat the butter, icing sugar and vanilla together in a bowl until light and fluffy, then beat in the milk.

Once the whoopies are completely cool, gently release them from the baking paper. Take a generous dollop of the buttercream and spread it onto the flat base of one of the whoopies, then sandwich it together with a second whoopie. Repeat with the rest of the cakes.

Variations
Vanilla: Omit the cocoa powder and add an extra 55g (2oz) of flour.
Coffee: Omit the cocoa powder and add an extra 55g (2oz) of flour, plus a few drops of coffee essence or 2 tablespooons of instant coffee powder stirred into the warmed milk.

Tangerine
Financier Cakes

Financier cakes are often served in restaurants as petit-fours. They are usually small, rectangular cakes with a nutty, zingy flavour and a light, spongy texture. Financier moulds can be found on the internet but otherwise a mini-muffin mould can be used instead. Makes 12, or more if you make mini ones *(V)*

Vegetable oil or oil spray, for oiling

80g (3oz) butter, melted

2 tsp golden syrup

130g (4½oz) icing sugar

60g (2¼oz) plain flour

1 tsp baking powder

Pinch of salt

60g (2¼oz) ground almonds

4 egg whites

Finely grated zest of 2 tangerines (or mandarins if you like)

Equipment

Financier mould

Preheat the oven to 180°C (350°F), Gas Mark 4 with the middle shelf ready. Oil a financier mould.

Melt the butter in a small pan, stir in the golden syrup and set aside. Sift together the icing sugar, flour, baking powder and salt, then stir in the ground almonds.

Whisk the egg whites together in a large bowl until they are white and frothy, but stop before they start to form peaks. Add the icing sugar, ground almonds, flour, salt and baking powder and mix with a metal spoon until well combined. Add the tangerine zest and fold together until uniform. Gradually pour in the melted butter and golden syrup, stirring all the time.

Spoon the mixture into the moulds, filling them two-thirds full. Bake in the oven for 10–15 minutes or until risen and spongy. Remove from the oven and leave in the moulds for a couple of minutes, then turn out onto a wire rack to cool completely.

Vanilla Tuiles

These light and crispy biscuits are a delight to enjoy. They can be tricky to make though, so I urge you to practise your technique, and to use an offset spatula, which makes spreading the batter thinly much easier. The tuilles can be stored for days. Serve with ice cream or sorbet, or mountains of mixed berries and crème fraîche. Alternatively, enjoy them simply with a cup of English Breakfast tea and your favourite read. *Makes 12 (V)*

Vegetable oil, for oiling (optional)

60g (2½oz) very soft butter

60g (2½oz) caster sugar

Few drops of vanilla extract

2 egg whites, lightly whisked

100g (3½oz) plain flour

Pinch of salt

Preheat the oven to 170°C (325°F), Gas Mark 3. Use a silicone mat, or line a baking tray with baking paper and oil lightly. Cut out cardboard stencils, about 8cm (3in) in size.

Put the butter, sugar and vanilla in a large bowl and cream together. Add half of the egg white and half the flour and stir to just combine, then add the salt, the rest of the egg white and the flour and mix well.

Put the stencil down on the baking paper, take a blob of the tuile mix and spread it over the cut out to make a thin layer. Pull off the stencil then repeat with the rest of the tuille batter. Bake in the oven for about 8 minutes, or until the tuiles are crisp. Remove the tuiles from the oven and leave to cool on the tray. Once cool, ease off with a palette knife.

Variation For chocolate tuiles, use 80g (3oz) plain flour and 20g (¾oz) cocoa powder.

Basics

Puff Pastry

The block of butter in this recipe is divided into two parts – the smaller bit should be chilled and the rest needs to be nice and soft. The best way to make it the right softness and shape is to put the butter between two sheets of greaseproof or baking paper and bash it with a rolling pin until pliable. Makes 615g (1lb 6oz) *(V)*

245g (8¾oz) plain flour, plus extra for dusting

½ tsp salt

40g (1½oz) butter, chilled and cubed

130ml (4½fl oz) cold water

210g (7½oz) butter, softened (see intro)

Put the flour, salt and chilled butter into a large bowl and rub them together with your fingertips until they resemble fine breadcrumbs. Make a well in the centre of the mixture and pour in the water. Mix with a knife, then bring the dough together with your hands.

Squidge into a ball, then wrap in clingfilm and put in the fridge for 25 minutes.

Unwrap the dough ball and use a knife to score a large cross in the middle of it, cutting no more than halfway through. Lift all four corners from the middle of the cross, then pull them up and out to make the cross big enough to put the softened butter into.

Add the butter, then fold the corners of the cross back to the centre, covering the butter so it is completely enclosed. The corners should overlap in the centre so no butter is showing. It is important that the butter is not too hard or too soft otherwise it will escape through the dough when you roll it out and the resulting pastry will not rise as well. If it's too hard, leave the ball of pastry at room temperature until the butter inside has softened; if it is getting too soft, pop it in the fridge for 20 minutes to firm up a little before rolling.

▶

This next process is called 'rolling and folding' (or 'turns') and it creates the characteristic flaky layers of puff pastry. Begin by rolling the pastry out away from you on a well-floured surface to a rectangle roughly 3 times as long as it is wide (don't turn the pastry when rolling). Keep the corners square and edges straight by pressing a palette knife or ruler against them. Lift the dough occasionally to make sure it isn't sticking; flour the work surface again if necessary and sprinkle with more flour as you go, dusting away any excess with a pastry brush. Take the short edge of the pastry nearest to you and fold it up a third, then fold the top edge down a third to give a rectangular block. Turn the dough 90° and then repeat the rolling and folding.

You have now given the dough two 'rolls and folds'. Wrap the dough in clingfilm and put in the fridge. Chill for 20 minutes.

Remove the dough from the fridge, unwrap and give it two more 'rolls and folds'. Wrap and rest in the fridge for at least another 20 minutes. The block of puff pastry can at this point be kept in the fridge for a day or two, or frozen.

Remove from the fridge, unwrap and give the dough a final couple of rolls and folds, then roll it out to the size desired for your chosen recipe. Place on a baking tray, cover with oiled clingfilm and leave to rest in the fridge for about 30 minutes before using.

Savoury & sweet
Shortcrust Pastry

Oh, go on. Give it a go! I know pastry is the nemesis of the average person's baking repertoire, but do try these recipes, even if just the once. This pastry is crumbly, buttery and completely lovely. The ingredients differ slightly for the savoury and sweet versions, so follow the list for the one you need, but the method is virtually the same. Makes about 500g (1lb 2oz) (V)

Savoury
shortcrust pastry

250g (9oz) plain flour

125g (4½oz) cold butter, cubed

2 egg yolks

Large pinch of salt

1–4 tbsp water, if needed

Sweet
shortcrust pastry

250g (9oz) plain flour

125g (4½oz) cold butter, cubed

2 egg yolks

2 tbsp caster sugar

Large pinch of salt

1–4 tbsp single cream or milk, if needed

Put the flour and butter in a food processor and blitz to breadcrumbs. If using your hands, rub the butter and flour together until the mixture resembles fine breadcrumbs. Add the egg yolks (and if making sweet pastry, the sugar) and a pinch of salt and stir together with a knife. Squidge the mixture together into a ball. If the pastry feels very dry add the water (or if making sweet pastry, the cream or milk), but try and get by without for a more tender pastry.

Once the pastry is all squidged together, pop it in the fridge to rest for 30 minutes.

After 30 minutes, remove it from the fridge and let it warm up a little (if you use it straight from the fridge and try to roll it out, the pastry will just be a hopeless crumbly mess). Roll the pastry out on a lightly floured board and use as required.

Thyme & Polenta
Pastry

I love pastry. I like making it from scratch and then using it in new and exciting recipes. This version has a comforting crumblyness to it, and is perfect for the top of a chicken pie, or around a sausage roll. It is also wonderful for the case of a creamy mushroom quiche. I would make this delicious version and allow it an hour in the fridge wrapped in clingfilm before using it. This prevents it from shrinking too much once it gets in the oven. Makes 415g (14½oz) (V)

180g (6½oz) plain flour, plus extra for dusting

Pinch of salt

60g (2¼oz) polenta (or other cornmeal)

115g (4oz) cold butter, cubed

Small handful of fresh thyme leaves

1–2 eggs, lightly beaten

Put the flour, salt, cornmeal and butter in a medium bowl, and using your fingers, rub the mixture together until it has consistency of large breadcrumbs. The easiest way to do this is in a food processor – a few sharp bursts and the mixture will be ready to go. Stir in the thyme with a knife, then add the egg and mix together quickly.

Scoop up the mixture from the bowl and knead on a lightly floured work surface for about 10 seconds, until smooth. Wrap in clingfilm and put in the fridge to rest for 30 minutes, then use as required.

Lemon & Almond
Pastry

Almondy, citrusy pastry. Simply angelic, and great used for Bakewell Tart (see page 112). Makes about 500g (1lb 2oz) *(V)*

115g (4oz) butter, softened

60g (2½oz) caster sugar

Seeds of 1 vanilla pod

Finely grated zest of 1 lemon

2 eggs, lightly beaten

200g (7oz) plain flour

Pinch of salt

45g (1½oz) ground almonds

Put the butter, sugar, vanilla and lemon zest in a bowl and beat until well combined. Beat in the egg yolks one at a time, then add the flour, salt and almonds and mix until the dough just starts to come together but is uniform.

Shape the dough into a round, wrap in clingfilm and put in the fridge to rest for 2 hours before use.

Coconut Pastry

Use this recipe as a change from sweet shortcrust. Although not as crumbly as shortcrust, it can still be a challenge, as the bits of coconut tend to cut through the dough, marking and splitting it. A coconut pastry case is delicious and filled with cream and bananas or other exotic fruit. Makes about 500g (1lb 2oz) *(V)*

2 egg yolks

Seeds from 1 vanilla pod or 2 tsp vanilla extract

100g (3½oz) caster sugar

100g (3½oz) butter, softened

165g (5½oz) plain flour, plus extra for dusting

60g (2½oz) unsweetened desiccated coconut

Pinch of salt

Put the egg yolks, vanilla, sugar and butter in a large bowl and cream together until pale and fluffy. Add the flour, coconut and salt and mix together until the dough begins to form large chunks. Using your hands, bring the mixture together, then remove from the bowl and knead it gently for 10 seconds on a lightly floured work surface. Wrap in clingfilm and put in the fridge to rest for 30 minutes. Roll the pastry out on a lightly floured board and use as required.

Chocolate crème
Patissière

A mischievous chocolate-cream filling often found in French pastries. Perhaps use it to fill doughnuts, Les Petit Croquembouche or instead of the lemon cream in the Blueberry Millefeuilles. Makes 500ml (18fl oz)

400ml (14fl oz) milk

100g (3½oz) good dark chocolate (at least 64% cocoa solids or more), grated or finely chopped

4 egg yolks

165g (5½oz) caster sugar

40g (1½oz) plain flour

Pinch of salt

Put a double layer of clingfilm on a plate so it overlaps the edges by about 30cm (12in).

Heat the milk in a small pan to just below boiling. Remove the pan from the heat and add the grated chocolate. Set aside and keep warm.

In a medium pan, mix the egg yolks, sugar, flour and salt until well combined. It will be a thick paste. Pour a few tablespoons of the chocolate milk into the egg and flour mixture and stir hard to get rid of any lumps then gradually add the rest of the chocolate milk, stirring hard all the time. If the mixture is lumpy, whisk hard for a minute or so.

Put the pan on a medium heat and heat through, stirring all the time. The mixture will begin to thicken, keep heating it until it is just about to boil then remove the pan from the heat and tip it on to the clingfilm. Leave to cool for a few minutes then fold the clingfilm over it to prevent a 'skin' from forming. Let it cool completely then put in the fridge and use within two days.

Vanilla crème
Patissière

Makes 500ml (18fl oz)

400ml (14fl oz) milk

Seeds of 1 vanilla pod or
2 drops of vanilla extract

3 egg yolks

80g (3½oz) caster sugar

40g (1½oz) plain flour

Pinch of salt

30g (1¼oz) butter

Put a double layer of clingfilm on a plate so it overlaps the edges by about 30cm (12in).

Heat the milk and vanilla in a small pan to just below boiling. Remove the pan from the heat, then set aside and keep warm.

In a medium pan, mix the egg yolks, sugar, flour and salt until well combined. It will be a thick paste. Pour a few tablespoons of the vanilla milk into the egg and flour mixture and stir hard to get rid of any lumps, then gradually add the rest of the milk, stirring hard all the time. If the mixture is lumpy, whisk hard for a minute or so.

Put the pan over a medium heat and heat through, stirring all the time. The mixture will begin to thicken. Keep heating it until it is just about to boil, then remove the pan from the heat and tip it on to the clingfilm. Dot the crème patissière with the butter and leave it to cool for a few minutes before folding the clingfilm over to prevent a 'skin' from forming. Let it cool completely then put in the fridge and use within two days.

Index &
Acknowledgments

Index

Acknowledgments

I would like to take this opportunity to thank everyone who has supported me through this exciting process:

The brilliant team of Paula Karaiskos, Sarah Doukas, Simon Chambers, Lou Grima and Emily Shanks for making my transition from catwalk to kitchen a smooth one.

The fabulous Rachel Purnell at Pacific, Lisa Edwards and the team at the BBC, the talented Myles New, the girls Xanna, Sophia, Olivia Ball and Carl, Ben the director extraordinaire, Orlando, Dave, Bridget, Jason, Sophie, Ben and Sharon Hearne Smith.

Carole Tonkinson and the team at HarperCollins for pulling the rabbit out of the hat and producing such a stunning book.

Velma Rowe, Tony Walker, Laurie Rose, Bob Carlos Clarke, Lindsay Carlos Clarke, Benjamin Christopherson, Polly Vernon, Tom Aikens, the brilliant Marco Pierre White, Rodney, the London Foodie supremo Ewan Venters, the witty William Sitwell, and my brilliant 'business team': Andrew Antonio, Mya Castillo, January, Spenta, Loic Battenoive and the boys, Alex Kabalin, Beverly Churchill and Ian Hawksworth, Rose Chorlton, Lydia, Fiaz and family.

My teachers Neil Armstrong, Yolande Stanley and Professor David Foskett, who helped my love of food to blossom.

My primary school teacher for showing me how to cook raspberry buns.

My family and my daughter Ella and my partner Ged.

Big love for being there through the twists and the turns of this culinary roller coaster, the late-night phone calls and pre-dawn emails. Thank you all so much for making this project possible.

LP xxx